Commercial and Economic Law in the United States of America

Table of Contents

List of Abbreviations

BIS	Bureau of Industry and Security
CBP	Customs and Border Protection
CCL	Commerce Control List
CFIUS	Committee on Foreign Investment in the United States
C.F.R.	Code of Federal Regulations
CFTC	Commodity Futures Trading Commission
CIF	Cost, insurance, freight
DOJ	Department of Justice
EAR	Export Administration Regulations
ECCN	Export Control Classification Number
FCPA	Foreign Corrupt Practices Act
FDA	Federal Drug Administration
FOB	Free on Board
FTC	Federal Trade Commission
HHI	Herfindahl-Hirschman Index
HIPAA	Health Insurance Portability and Accountability Act
HSR Act	Hart-Scott-Rodino Antitrust Improvements Act
LLC	Limited Liability Companies
NCCUSL	National Conference of Commissioners on Uniform State Laws
SEC	Securities and Exchange Commission
U.S.C.	United States Code
UCC	Uniform Commercial Code
UTSA	Uniform Trade Secrets Act
VARA	Visual Artists Rights Act

List of Abbreviations

General Introduction

§1. GENERAL BACKGROUND OF THE UNITED STATES

I. Geography

1. The United States (U.S.), which comprises 9,629,091 km^2 of territory (including water), is the world's third largest country by geographic size (after Russia and Canada). It shares a common border with only two countries: Canada and Mexico. The lowest point in the country is in Death Valley and is 86 m below sea level. The highest point is Mount McKinley at 6,194 m above sea level. Approximately 19% of its land is arable.

II. Demography

2. The population of the U.S. in 2018 was 326 million with 49% male and 51% female. The population is growing at an annual rate of approximately 0.77%.

III. Cultural Composition

3. The U.S. is often described as a melting pot. The term melting pot refers to the fact that the U.S. is comprised of individuals whose forefathers or themselves immigrated from overseas. Today, the largest immigrant population is Hispanic. It is therefore difficult to speak of a common culture in the U.S. Over 2% of the total population considers itself to be of two or more races.

4. According to figures of the U.S. Census Bureau for the year 2017, the ethnic composition of the U.S. population is as follows:

- white: 66.2%;
- black: 13.1%;
- Asian: 4.2%;
- American Indian, Eskimo Aleut: 1.1%;
- Hispanic: 16.2%.

5. The population of the country is 56% Protestant, 28% Roman Catholic, and 2% Jewish.

IV. Political System

A. *Branches of Government*

6. The U.S. Constitution establishes a federal government comprised of three "branches": the executive, legislative, and judicial. The relationship between the branches is characterized by a system of checks and balances. This essentially means that each branch has certain powers over the others. For example, the Executive Branch has the authority to veto legislation of the Legislative Branch. The Legislative Branch acts as a check over the Executive Branch when, for example, it must seek the approval of the Legislative Branch for international treaties. The system of checks and balances is a manifestation of the general mistrust of government that was predominant at the time the Constitution was drafted. This mistrust still exists in social, economic, and legal context. The notions of individualism, free market capitalism, and freedom of contract are more readily apparent in the U.S. than in most other countries.

B. *Executive Branch*

7. The Executive Branch is comprised of the President and all the individuals, agencies, and departments that report to the President. The role of the Executive Branch of the government is to administer and enforce the laws of the U.S. In addition to its enforcement powers, the Executive Branch also has the authority to promulgate rules in certain areas. The President serves as the head of the Executive Branch of government and the chief of state. The President is elected every four years. The Executive Branch is comprised of the Executive Office of the President, the Cabinet that is appointed by the President with Senate approval, and a large number of federal agencies and departments.

C. *Legislative Branch*

8. The legislative power of the federal government is conferred by the Constitution on Congress. Its authority is limited by the doctrine of enumerated powers. This doctrine provides that Congress has only those authorities that are specifically enumerated in the U.S. Constitution. In particular, Congress has the power under the Constitution (Article III section 8), to assess and collect taxes, to regulate commerce with foreign nations and between states, to coin money, to establish post offices, to establish courts inferior to the Supreme Court, to declare war, to establish rules for the government, and to raise and maintain an army and navy. In addition, the Constitution gives Congress the "catch-all" authority to make laws that are necessary and proper for executing the powers that the Constitution specifically grants to it.

9. Congress is composed of two chambers: the Senate and the House of Representatives. The Senate comprises 100 senators—two being elected by each state.

The larger chamber, the House of Representatives, comprises 435 representatives apportioned among the states in relation to the population of the particular state.

D. *Judicial Branch*

10. The Judicial Branch is comprised of the U.S. Supreme Court and the federal courts created by Congress based on Article III of the Constitution. At the top of the Judicial Branch of the government is the U.S. Supreme Court comprised of nine justices (one chief justice and eight associate justices). The justices are nominated by the President and confirmed by the Senate. Their terms last until they retire or are impeached by Congress. The "check" that the Supreme Court has over the Legislative Branch is its power of judicial review. However, this power, which means that the Supreme Court can review acts of the Legislative Branch, is not specifically granted by the Constitution. Rather, it rests on an unwritten consensus that has its roots in the famous case *Marbury v. Madison.*[1] In that case, the Supreme Court held that it had the authority to review acts of Congress based on rights "inferred" from the Constitution. This does not mean, however, that the power of the Supreme Court is unchecked. Congress not only has the right to impeach the justices but the Constitution can be amended with approval of three-fourths of the states.

E. *Political Parties*

11. There are two main political parties that dominate the political landscape in the U.S.: the Democratic Party and the Republican Party. In the 2016 Presidential election, the Democratic and Republican parties together received 94.3% of the popular vote (Republicans 46.1% and Democrats 48.2%).

V. The Economic System

12. The U.S. economic system is commonly referred to as capitalistic. This is not entirely correct. Although the U.S. economic system relies for a large extent on market forces to determine the allocation of scarce resources, there is a fair amount of state intervention. The 2017 gross domestic product of the U.S. was USD $19.391 trillion (1.6% agriculture, 18.9% industry, and 78.4% services). At that time, 12.7% of the population was living below the poverty level. Managerial and professional occupations comprise 26.2% of the labor force with technical, sales and administrative support (38.3%), services (19.2%), manufacturing, mining, transportation and crafts (18.1%) and farming, forestry and fishing (0.9%) comprising the rest.

1. 5 U.S. 1 (Cranch) (1803).

13. The primary exports from the U.S. are civilian aircrafts, medical supplies, industrial machines and equipment, and automotive parts. The leading export destinations based upon 2017 figures are Mexico ($243 billion), China ($130.4 billion) and the UK ($56.3 billion).

VI. The Legal System

A. Sources of Law

14. There are various sources of law in the U.S. legal system including the federal and state constitutions, treaties with foreign states, federal state, and local laws and the common law (i.e., precedents).[2] The U.S. Constitution is the highest source of law in the U.S. legal system. The Constitution was ratified in 1788 and contains seven articles and twenty-six amendments. The first ten amendments are referred to as the Bill of Rights.

15. The provisions of the Constitution fall into one of the following categories:

- provisions that identify and delegate power to the three branches of government;
- provisions that delineate the separation of power and govern the system of checks and balances upon which the system of government rests;
- provisions reserving power to the states vis-à-vis the federal government; and
- provisions that enumerate the fundamental rights held by the citizens.

16. In 1776, the thirteen British colonies declared their independence from Britain. Despite this "Declaration of Independence," the British Empire continued to influence many aspects of society. One aspect of society that continued to be influenced was the legal system. With the exception of the state of Louisiana, which later joined the union, the U.S. has a common law legal system similar in many ways to the legal systems of the other British colonies.

17. In abstract terms, the common law consists of those principles and rules embodied in case law rather than any legislative enactments. The term has its origins in the medieval understanding that law, as determined by the regent, represented the common will of the people. The common law system as it exists in the U.S. today is really a combination of case law and statute. Indeed, much of the law applicable to commercial conduct is based on statute. In the event of a conflict between a statute and common law, the statute will prevail based on the notion that it reflects the will of the people. Nonetheless, case law is important in this context to the extent that it provides guidance to the meaning of the statute.

2. John B. Attanasio, *Understanding Constitutional Law* (4th ed., 2012).

B. The Doctrine of Stare Decisis

18. The U.S. common law system rests on the doctrine of stare decisis. In most, if not all, legal systems judicial decisions are a source of the law. What distinguishes a common law system is that judicial decisions are not only a source of the law but they are also the law. A judge must follow the decisions of higher courts unless that judge can distinguish the case before him or her from the prior decision.[3] This is known as the doctrine of stare decisis. It basically means that like facts will receive like treatment in a court of law. Even the Supreme Court will not depart from the doctrine of stare decisis without some compelling justification.[4]

19. The doctrine of stare decisis serves many of the same principles as the doctrine of legal certainty in civil law systems.[5] It is, however, not absolute. As the Supreme Court stated in *State Oil Co. v. Khan*, stare decisis reflects a policy judgment that in most matters it is more important that the applicable rule of law be settled than that it be settled right.[6] According to the Supreme Court, if the application of stare decisis perpetuates a wrong statutory interpretation, "critics of our ruling can take their objections across the street, and Congress can correct any mistake it sees."[7]

C. Relationship Between State and Federal Law

20. The "supremacy clause" of the U.S. Constitution (Article VI) provides that the Constitution and the laws that are made in pursuance of the Constitution are the supreme law of the U.S. In the event of a conflict between state and federal law, federal law takes precedence only if the state law stands as an obstacle to the accomplishment and execution of the purposes and objectives of the federal statute.[8] The states may extend greater protection to individuals and businesses than the U.S. Constitution grants.[9]

D. Limited Power of Federal Government

21. The powers of the federal government are limited. The general principle is that all power that is not specifically granted to Congress by the Constitution is reserved for the states. However, the Constitution identifies certain areas in which the states may not act, for example, concluding international agreements with foreign nations (Article I, section 10).

3. *Kimble v. Marvel Entertainment*, LLC, 135 S.Ct. 2401, 2409 (2015).
4. *Hilton v. South Carolina Public Railways Comm'n*, 502 U.S. 197 (1991).
5. *Payne v. Tennessee*, 501 U.S. 808, 827-28 (1991).
6. 118 S.Ct. 275 (1997).
7. *Kimble v. Marvel Entertainment*, LLC, 135 S.Ct. 2401, 2409 (2015).
8. *Jones v. Rath Packing*, 430 U.S. 519, 526 (1976).
9. *Prune Yard Shopping Center v. Robins*, 447 U.S. 74 (1980).

22. This limitation on the authority of the federal government is not as strict as it may initially appear. As discussed above, the federal government has only those authorities that are specifically enumerated in the Constitution. One such enumerated authority is the "power to regulate commerce among the several states."[10] This is referred to as the "Commerce Clause." In theory, this would simply seem to suggest that the federal government can regulate trade between states. However, the Supreme Court has given a much broader interpretation to the Commerce Clause. Even where the effect of a particular activity has a remote effect on interstate trade, the Supreme Court has found federal regulation of that activity to be legitimate. It has even held that Congress has the authority to regulate a family farm that produces and consumes its own wheat.[11]

VII. Judicial System

A. Federal Court System

23. The U.S. Constitution establishes a Supreme Court with limited jurisdiction.[12] It has "original jurisdiction" over cases involving a state as a party or affecting ambassadors or public servants or appeals from decisions of a Supreme Court of a state.

24. The U.S. Constitution also empowers the Legislative Branch to establish lower federal courts to hear all other types of cases. The jurisdiction of these federal courts is strictly limited. They only have jurisdiction to hear cases arising under the laws and treaties of the U.S. and the U.S. Constitution (commonly referred to as "federal question jurisdiction") or involving the U.S. as a party and cases between citizens of different states or between citizen of the U.S. and a citizen of a foreign country (commonly referred to as "diversity jurisdiction").[13]

25. The federal court system has three levels. The federal Courts of First Instance are referred to as the federal district courts that are divided geographically throughout the U.S. Each state has at least one federal court but no state has more than four. Each district court has at least two judges. In addition, there are several specialty courts that also act as Courts of First Instance but whose jurisdiction is delineated by subject matter: Court of Federal Claims, Court of International Trade, U.S. Tax Court, and so on.

26. The districts are organized into twelve circuits. The courts with jurisdiction within these courts are commonly referred to as Courts of Appeal. In addition, there is the Court of Appeals for the Federal Circuit that hears appeals from the Court of

---

10. Constitution Art. I s. 8.
11. *Wickard v. Filburn*, 317 U.S. 111 (1942).
12. Linda Mullenix, *Understanding Federal Courts and Jurisdiction* (1998).
13. Congress has added the further requirement that the amount in controversy in diversity cases must be USD 75,000 or greater (28 U.S.C. §1332).

International Trade, the Court of Federal Claims, the Patent and Trademark Office and the various administrative agencies. Appeals of decisions of the Courts of Appeal can be made to the U.S. Supreme Court.

B. State Court System

27. In addition to the federal judicial system, each of the fifty states has its own judicial system independent from the federal system. The particular structure of the state court system is determined by the particular state's constitution and statutes. Most states have a tri-level judicial system with a trial court, an appellate court, and a Supreme Court. Only eight states have a bi-level judicial system. The jurisdiction of the state courts is considered to be general (as opposed to the limited jurisdiction of the federal courts). In other words, the state courts have jurisdiction over all cases except those that are in the exclusive jurisdiction of the federal courts. If a case falls within the nonexclusive jurisdiction of the federal courts, for example, a diversity case, both the federal and state courts may have parallel jurisdiction. Many states have special courts to deal with particularly complex cases or cases where there are benefits to having an experienced judge to adjudicate the dispute.

Part I. Commercial Law

Chapter 1. Concepts and Sources of Commercial Law

§1. The Distinction between Tort and Contract Law

28. The U.S. legal system makes an important distinction between tort law and contract law. Tort law generally involves legal wrongs committed by one person to another person independent of contract. It is based on certain standards of conduct and responsibilities imposed by the law on individuals. Negligence, for example, is a tort law claim. Contract law, however, is concerned only with rights and obligations between persons created by agreement. A breach of that agreement gives rise to a contractual claim. However, certain torts, such as intentional interference with a contractual relationship, may be "in tort" even though they involve a breach of contract.

29. The strict adherence to the distinction between contract and tort law can have curious results. For example, the traditional rule is that an injured plaintiff cannot receive punitive damages[14] for claims based only on contract. Punitive damages are only awarded for tort claims.[15] Therefore, a party to a contract may intentionally breach that contract without the fear of having to pay punitive damages to the injured party.

§2. Constitutional Law

30. The highest source of commercial law is the U.S. Constitution. The U.S. Constitution is important in the context of commercial law in two respects. First, the U.S. Constitution is a source of fundamental rights and liberties of U.S. citizens. This includes, to a limited extent, economic liberties. Second, it is also a source of limitations of the ability of the federal government to regulate certain activities. For example, the U.S. Constitution may prevent the government from regulating certain commercial activity and activities of companies.[16]

---

14. Punitive damages are those damages awarded to the plaintiff above and beyond compensation for the injury suffered by the plaintiff.
15. *See*, e.g., *Ronald E. Morrow v. L.A. Goldschmidt Associates*, 492 N.E.2d 181 (1986).
16. *Citizens United v. Federal Election Commission*, 558 U.S. 310 (2010).

§3. Statutory Law

31. Statutory law is the most important source of commercial law in the U.S. This ranges from general laws such as the Uniform Commercial Code (UCC) to laws applicable to specific sections of the economy. Statutory law refers to both the plethora of federal laws adopted by Congress as well as the legislation adopted by the state and local governments.

32. An understanding of commercial law in the U.S. requires a brief discussion of the UCC. The UCC is a code of laws drafted by the National Conference of Commissioners on Uniform State Laws (NCCUSL) and the American Law Institute. It addresses not only sales transactions but also commercial paper, letters of credit, bulk transfers, bills of lading, investment securities, and secured transactions. Although it is not a law itself, its provisions have been adopted in whole or in part by all of the U.S. states.

§4. Common Law

33. As discussed above, the U.S. legal system is based on common law. The common law is generally the law determined by the cases. Nonetheless, as discussed above, the field of commercial law is primarily governed by statutory law. Cases continue to be relevant because they determine how the commercial law statutes are interpreted and applied.

§5. International Law

34. In the U.S., international treaties and conventions are an important source of commercial law.[17] For example, the U.S. has signed and ratified the United Nations Convention on the International Sale of Goods.[18] This law is now part of the U.S. legal system. The convention applies to contracts of sale of goods between parties whose places of business are in different countries provided that those countries have adopted the convention or the rules of private international law lead to the application of the law of a contracting state.

---

17. For a discussion of the status of international law in the U.S. legal system *see* Paul Dubinsky, International Law in the Legal System of the United States, 58 Am. J. Comp. L. 455 (2010); Stephen McCaffrey, *Understanding International Law* 127–137 (Matthew Bender 2d ed. 2015).
18. Final Act of the United Nations Conference on Contracts for the International Sale of Goods, Apr. 10, 1980, U.N. Doc. A/CONF.97/18 (1980), reprinted in S. Treaty Doc. No. 98-9, (1983) and 19 I.L.M. 668.

Chapter 2. Economic Operators

§1. Merchants

35. In the U.S., the UCC defines a merchant as: "a person who deals in goods of the kind or otherwise by his occupation holds himself out as having knowledge or skill peculiar to the practices or goods involved in the transaction" (UCC section 2-104(1)). The definition makes it clear that a person does not necessarily have to be a seller of a good to be considered a merchant. A bank that used microfilming equipment in its business was considered a merchant because of its familiarity with the good.[19] The significance of this definition in U.S. law is that certain provisions of the UCC apply only to transactions between merchants (UCC section 2-201(2)) or if one party is a merchant (UCC section 2-314). In addition, in certain contexts a merchant is held to a higher standard than non-merchants.

§2. Natural Persons

I. Persons

36. U.S. business law also employs the concept of "person." For example, the antitrust laws generally apply only to "persons." This would preclude, for example, the application of the antitrust laws to the federal government.[20]

II. Minors

37. The term "minor" is generally used to describe a person who is under the age of legal competence. The common law rule is that a contract entered into by a minor is not void but is voidable by the minor. The precise age under which a person is considered to be a minor depends on the particular statute that is at issue. The common law threshold age is 21. However, in most states, a person under the age of 18 is considered to be a minor.

III. Aliens

38. The concept of an "alien" is defined in relation to the particular legal norm in which the concept is employed. For example, the term "alien" as used in the Immigration and Nationality Act means any person not a citizen or national of the U.S. (8 U.S.C. section 1101(a)(3)). Aliens lawfully residing in the U.S. are generally entitled to the protection of the laws with regard to their person or property.[21]

---

19. *National Microsales Corp. v. Chase Manhattan Bank*, 761 F.Supp. 304 (1991).
20. *United States v. Cooper*, 312 U.S. 600 (1941).
21. *Carlson v. Landon*, 342 U.S. 524 (1952); *US v. Winter*, 509 F.2d 975 (1975).

The Supreme Court has held that aliens lawfully residing in the U.S. have the same rights to enter into and enforce contracts as citizens.[22]

IV. Citizens

39. The concept of alien is used in contradistinction to the terms "citizen" and "nationals." The term "national" of the U.S. means a citizen of the U.S. or a person who, though not a citizen of the U.S., owes permanent allegiance to the U.S. (8 U.S.C. section 1101(a)(22)).

40. A person becomes both a national and a citizen of the U.S. at birth if he or she is born in the U.S. (8 U.S.C. section 1401(a)). However, a person born outside of the U.S. may also be a national and citizen of the U.S. if that person's parents are both citizens of the U.S. and at least one has had a residence in the U.S. prior to the birth of such person, or at least one of that person's parents is a citizen of the U.S. and that parent has been physically present in the U.S. for a continuous period of one year prior to the birth of such person and the other parent is a national, but not a citizen, of the U.S. If the person is born outside the U.S. to parents one of whom is an alien and the other a citizen of the U.S. who, prior to the birth of such person, was physically present in the U.S. for a period or periods totaling not less than five years, at least two of which were after attaining the age of 14 years, that person will be considered a national and citizen of the U.S. (8 U.S.C. section 1401(g)).

41. In addition, it is possible to become a national by birth (but not a citizen). For example, a person born outside the U.S. to parents both of whom are nationals, but not citizens, of the U.S., and have had a residence in the U.S. prior to the birth of such person is a national (but not a citizen) of the U.S. (8 U.S.C. section 1408(2)).

42. The fundamental incident of U.S. citizenship is the absolute and unqualified right to residence within the U.S.[23] However, this is the only absolute and unqualified right conferred by citizenship. For example, the status of citizen does not necessarily mean that the person is entitled to vote.[24]

V. Agents

43. The status of agent describes a fiduciary relationship by which one party (i.e., the agent) is empowered to act on behalf of another (i.e., the principal). Agency, according to the U.S. Supreme Court, is the fiduciary relationship that results from the manifestation of consent by one person to another that the other

22. *Torao Takahashi v. Fish and Game Commission*, 334 U.S. 410 (1948).
23. *US v. Valentine*, 288 F.Supp. 957 (1968).
24. *Sanchez v. US*, 376 F.Supp. 239 (1974).

shall act on his or her behalf and subject to his or her control, and consent by the other so to act.[25] An agent may be a natural person or a legal person.

44. There are three types of agency: "general," "universal," and "special." A general agent is authorized to do all acts connected with the business or employment in which that agent is engaged. A special agent is authorized to do only specific acts in pursuance of specific instructions or restrictions. A universal agent is authorized to transact all the business of the principal and do all delegable acts for such principal.

45. The status of agent should be distinguished from that of an independent contractor. An independent contractor is a person who contracts with another to do something for him or her, but who is not controlled by the other with respect to the performance of the assigned task. It is possible to be both an agent and an independent contractor. A person who contracts to act on behalf of another and subject to the other's control is an agent and also an independent contractor.[26]

46. The agency relationship generally exists only if there has been a manifestation of intent by the principal to the agent that the agent may act on the principal's account, and the agent has consented to accept such status. The valid creation of an agency relationship does not require consideration. Agency may result from a contract between the parties or it may result from a direction by a person to another to act on his or her account without an understanding that the other is to receive compensation for his or her services if he or she does act.[27]

47. The authority of the agent to act on behalf of the principal is one of the most important aspects of agency. Unless otherwise agreed, authority to conduct a transaction includes authority to do acts that are incidental to it, usually accompany it, or are reasonably necessary to accomplish it.[28] This is referred to as the "incidental authority" of the agent. The principal has the power to revoke the agent's authority even if this would constitute a breach of the contract between them.[29] The agency relationship lasts until it is terminated. Authority exists only during the period in which the agent reasonably believes that the principal desires him or her to act.

48. The principal may be liable to third parties in contract or tort law for actions of his or her agent. A person conducting an activity through servants or other agents is subject to liability for harm resulting from his or her conduct if he or she is negligent or reckless in giving improper or ambiguous orders, or in the supervision of the activity.

25. *NLRB v. Town & Country Elec. Inc.*, 516 U.S. 85 (1995).
26. Restatement Agency (Third) §14N.
27. *Id.*, §16.
28. *Id.*, §35.
29. *Id.*, §14.

49. The fact that an agent acts outside the scope of her authority does not necessarily mean that the obligations entered into by the agent are not binding on the principal. In certain circumstances, the principal can acquiesce to the conduct of the agent and thereby establish a binding effect where one would have otherwise not occurred. Acquiescence by the principal in a series of acts by the agent indicates authorization to perform similar acts in the future.[30]

VI. Master and Servant

50. The relationship between a master and servant (i.e., employer and employee) in U.S. law has many of the same characteristics as the relationship between a principal and agent. In fact, a "master" is a type of principal who employs a "servant" to perform service in his or her affairs and who controls or has the right to control the physical conduct of the other in the performance of service. The term "master" refers to the person who not only controls the results of the work of another person but also may direct the manner in which such work shall be completed. The rules applicable generally to principal and agent as to the creation of the relation, delegability, and capacity of the parties apply to master and servant.

51. The relationship of "master and servant" exists where an employer has the right to direct and control the method and manner in which work shall be done and results to be accomplished. By contrast, an "independent contractor" is one who engages to perform services for another according to his own method and manner, free from direction in the performance of work except as to the result of the work.[31]

VII. Independent Contractors

52. Whether the relationship is that of an "independent contractor" or "master and servant" depends on whether the entity for whom work is being performed has reserved a right of control over the means by which work is done. It is the reservation of the right of control by the principal, and not the actual exercise of such control, that governs the status of a relationship.[32] If the contractor possesses the right to direct the manner in which work is performed by the other party, there is "master–servant relationship." But if the contractor is only interested in the end result and retains no right to supervise manner of performance, the other party is an "independent contractor."[33]

30. *Id.*, §43.
31. *Long v. Valley Steel Products Co.*, 207 F.2d 505, 508 (1953).
32. *Shaw v. C.B. & E., Inc.*, 630 So.2d 401, 403 (1993).
33. *Kamm v. Morgan*, 157 So.2d 118,122 (1963).

VIII. Consumer

53. Although the common law does not recognize a formal category for consumers, there are a number of statutes in the U.S.—both federal and state—that rely on this concept. By way of example, the federal Magnuson-Moss Consumer Warranty Act defines a consumer as "a buyer other than for purposes of resale" (15 U.S.C. section 2301(3)). In contrast to the UCC definition of "merchant," the subjective knowledge of the person is not relevant.[34]

§3. Legal Persons

I. Sole Proprietorship

54. The sole proprietorship is the most prevalent form of doing business in the U.S. In general terms it is an individual operating a business. The sole proprietorship is not registered as a business entity. Moreover, there are no statutes governing its formation or operation. However, some states require the registration of any assumed name under which the proprietorship may operate.

55. The proprietor does business in his or her own name and for his or her own account. In other words, the proprietor assumes unlimited liability for the debts of the proprietorship. Despite its simplicity, this "flow-through" liability is the main disadvantage of the proprietorship.

II. Partnerships

56. The term "partnership" describes an arrangement whereby two or more persons agree to do business together. In general there are three types of partnerships in the U.S.: general partnerships, limited partnerships, and limited liability partnerships. General partnerships are governed by state law modeled on the Uniform Partnership Act. Limited partnerships are also governed by state law but these state laws are modeled on the Uniform Limited Partnership Act.

57. All partnerships must be based on an "association" between two or more persons. This requirement is generally fulfilled by the existence of an agreement between the partners to associate in a business relationship. Since sole proprietorships are limited to one person, the partnership structure has the advantage of the possibility to raise new capital by including additional partners.

58. The fundamental difference between a general partnership on the one hand and limited partnerships and limited liability partnerships on the other hand concerns the liability of the partners. In a general partnership, each of the partners remains personally liable for the debts of the partnership. If the partnership assets

34. *Karshan v. Mattituck Inlet Marina & Shipyard Inc.*, 785 F.Supp. 363 (1992).

are insufficient to satisfy the claims of creditors, the creditors may seek to satisfy their claims against the assets of the general partners. In practice, there are a number of ways the partners can shield their assets. This includes using a corporation as a partner, acquiring insurance and creating contractual arrangements to protect a partner.

59. The structure of limited partnerships and limited liability partnerships is similar to that of a general partnership. However, in limited partnerships and limited liability partnerships, the personal liability of at least one of the partners is limited and the liability of at least one of the other partners is unlimited. Because of the limited liability, the formation, registration, and operation of limited partnerships are governed by state statute. Thus, a limited partnership exists as a recognized legal entity after it has been properly registered as such with the appropriate statutory authority.

60. Another important distinction between a general partnership and to two forms of limited partnerships is the limitations on the managerial activities of the partners. The general rule is that the limited partner must remain the "silent" partner (i.e., she cannot participate in the management of the partnership). The limited partnership is therefore appropriate only where at least one partner is a passive investor.

III. Corporations

61. Corporations can be distinguished from partnerships in several respects. Perhaps the most basic distinguishing characteristic is that corporations are legal entities that exist separate from their incorporators and owners. As a separate legal entity with the ability to assume legal obligations, the incorporators and shareholders of the corporation are not generally liable for the corporation's debts. This "corporate veil" can, however, be pierced if the corporation merely acts as the alter ego of the owners or to avoid fraud.

62. Although the separateness of the corporation is advantageous from the perspective of protecting its shareholders, it is disadvantageous from a tax perspective. The separate status of the corporation means that the income of the corporation is taxed as well as the income that is distributed to the corporation's owners. However, subchapter S of the Internal Revenue Code allows a corporation to elect "subchapter S status" so that it is not taxed at the corporate level. This tax advantage has introduced a common distinction in the U.S. legal vernacular between "S corporations" and "C corporations." An "S corporation" is one that has met the requirements of subchapter S of the Internal Revenue Code and has elected subchapter S status. All other corporations are considered "C corporations." The distinction between S corporations and C corporations is relevant only from a tax perspective. From a commercial perspective, there is little importance to the distinction.

63. There are several important limitations on the ability of a corporation to elect subchapter S status. Nonresident aliens may not be shareholders in a subchapter S corporation. In addition, only individuals, estates, and trusts may be shareholders. Finally, a subchapter S corporation may only have one class of stock.

64. A large number of states have adopted legislation permitting the formation of a "close corporation." The close corporation is available in those cases where the investors are active in running the corporation rather than as mere passive investors. The qualification as a close corporation will depend on the particular rules of the state of incorporation. As a general rule, however, close corporation status is limited to those corporations that a small number of shareholders and whose shares are not publicly traded. In Delaware, for example, the maximum number of shareholders is thirty (section 342 Delaware General Corporation Law).

65. In order to prevent individuals engaged in certain professions from shielding themselves from personal liability through the vehicle of a corporation, the law prevented them from incorporating. This included lawyers, doctors, accountants, architects, and engineers. Now, however, all states allow for the existence of professional corporations. In most instances, the scope of the business must be limited to the particular profession and the shareholders must all be authorized to practice that profession.

66. The law applicable to the creation and operation of nonprofit corporations is state law. All states allow for the creation of nonprofit corporations. Nonprofit corporations are similar to for-profit corporations in that they are required to file organization papers with the state and comply with the applicable state laws. The fundamental difference between a for-profit and a nonprofit corporation is that the latter may not distribute income to its shareholders. In fact, the defining characteristic of nonprofit corporations is the lack of profit. This does not mean, however, that the nonprofit corporation is precluded from making a profit provided that the profit stays within the corporation to pay suppliers and employees. The income generated by nonprofit corporations is not taxed. Moreover, contributions to nonprofit corporations are generally tax deductible under the federal and state tax laws (26 U.S.C. section 501).

67. At least since the Michigan Supreme Court case of *Dodge v. Ford*, the purpose of the corporation was to serve its shareholders.[35] This notion of "shareholder primacy" came under scrutiny in the 1990s. There was an increased focus on the social context of the corporation. This "social enterprise movement" resulted in numerous states adopting social enterprise statutes. In some states such as Illinois, Michigan, North Carolina, Utah, Vermont, and Wyoming, this has taken the form of low-profit limited liability companies (LLC) (often referred to as "L3C companies"). In other states such as California, Illinois, Maryland, Massachusetts, New

35. *Dodge v. Ford Mottor Co.*, 170 N.W. 668 (Mich. 1919).

Jersey, and New York, this has taken the form of benefit corporations. The third type of social enterprise is the flexible purpose corporation.[36]

68. Although the various statutes differ in their details, their basic distinguishing characteristic, in contrast to traditional corporations or LLCs, is the recognition that the corporation owes duties not only to its owners but also the public or other stakeholders. Under traditional corporate law, courts have used a profit-maximization assumption to scrutinize decisions of corporate fiduciaries: Was the decision of the corporate fiduciary reasonably likely to maximize the profit for the corporation and hence the owners?[37] According to these new social enterprise statutes, corporate entities may take into account not only profit but also ancillary consequences of its decision such as the environment or employment. In Illinois, for example, the board of directors of a benefit corporation, in considering the best interests of the benefit corporation, may take into account the interests of the employees and workforce, the interests of customers as beneficiaries of the general public benefit, community and societal considerations, and the local and global environment.[38]

IV. Limited Liability Companies

69. The LLC is a relatively new form of legal entity in the U.S.[39] The first LLC statute was enacted in Wyoming in 1977 (Wyoming Statutes section 17-15-100). The LLC has limited liability characteristics similar to a corporate entity and the flow-through tax benefits similar to a partnership. The owners of an LLC are referred to the members. Each of them owns "membership interests" in that LLC. The LLC is managed by individuals who may or may not be members of the LLC. Competition between the states to attract business has resulted in LLC statutes being adopted in all fifty U.S. states.[40]

36. *See*, e.g., California Corp. Code s. 2500 (2013).
37. *Revlon, Inc. v. MacAndrews & Forbes Holdings, Inc.*, 506 A.2d 173 (Del. 1986).
38. 805 ILCS § 40/4.01.
39. William J. Carney, *Limited Liability Companies: Origins and Antecedents*, 6 *U. Colo. L. Rev.* 855 (1995).
40. Carol R. Goforth, *The Rise of the Limited Liability Company: Evidence of a Race Between the States, But Heading Where?*, 45 *Syracuse L. Rev.* 1271 (1995).

Chapter 3. Economic Institutions

§1. Private Institutions

I. Trade Associations

70. There is a plethora of trade associations active in the U.S. economy. Generally, these are divided among the professions and industries. Membership tends not to be compulsory.

II. Chambers of Commerce

71. In addition to the trade associations, there are numerous chambers of commerce both at the local, regional, and state level. In general terms, the primary function of these entities is to attract and assist businesses within the geographic area that they cover. In addition, the various chambers of commerce often promote the interests of their members by supporting legislation.

III. Better Business Bureau

72. The Better Business Bureau, which was founded in 1912, is a private organization with over 250,000 members nationwide. Its fundamental purpose is to promote fair and honest relationships between businesses and consumers. The Better Business Bureau serves as a private mechanism by which consumers can seek recourse against businesses. It also serves as a filter for many consumers. There is the perception that businesses that are members of the Better Business Bureau are more transparent in their business practices.

§2. Public Institutions

I. Commercial Courts

73. With some minor exceptions, the U.S. legal system does not have specialty courts as is common in other legal systems. The federal and state courts have jurisdiction over a wide range of issues from criminal to commercial claims. There are, however, several exceptions to this rule. Because of the complexities of the legal issues involved, the federal court system has created special courts for bankruptcy, customs, and tax.

74. The U.S. Bankruptcy Courts are integrated into the federal district courts. They have jurisdiction to apply the federal bankruptcy code (11 U.S.C. section 101). Appeals of decisions of the bankruptcy courts are heard by the respective federal district courts.

75. The U.S. Court of Federal Claims (formerly the Court of Claims) has jurisdiction over claims against the U.S. based on the federal Constitution, federal laws or contracts. The U.S. Court of International Trade (formerly the Customs Court), as its name suggests, has jurisdiction over customs cases. It also has the authority to review decisions of the Patent and Trademark Office.

76. The U.S. Tax Court was initially a part of the Executive Branch. It is currently an independent court with responsibility for claims involving the application of the U.S. federal tax laws by the Internal Revenue Service.

77. Similar to the federal courts, the court systems of the individual states do not generally have specialized commercial courts. One exception to this is the Commercial Division of the Supreme Court of the State of New York. In 1995, New York established this specialized court to handle commercial disputes.

II. Small Business Administration

78. The federal Small Business Administration was established by the federal government for the purpose of assisting small businesses throughout the U.S. It achieves this objective in several ways. In addition to providing basic information to entrepreneurs, the Small Business Administration guarantees short- and long-term loans to start-ups and existing companies. For example, the Export Working Capital Program of the Small Business Administration guarantees up to 90% of loans for export sales by small U.S. businesses. The Small Business Administration also provides business counseling and training. Participation in the various programs sponsored by the Small Business Administration is generally based on the size of the entity.

III. Commercial Arbitration

79. The U.S. legal system does not have courts of arbitration. With the exception of some state agencies offering arbitration services, the main arbitration institutions are private. The American Arbitration Association, for example, is one of the leading nonprofit organizations offering arbitration services. In addition, there are numerous private, for-profit organizations that offer such services, for example, JAMS/Endispute, United States Arbitration & Mediation, and Advanced Dispute Resolution, Inc.

80. As discussed above, there are no public courts of arbitration in the U.S. Alternative dispute resolution in the U.S. is left to private organizations. Alternative dispute resolution generally refers to arbitration and mediation. The general rule is that alternative dispute resolution is voluntary. Most types of legal disputes may be settled by alternative dispute resolution. It is not clear under U.S. law whether a court can require the parties to engage in alternative dispute resolution. Some courts have exercised such power[41] while others require an express statutory mandate to require alternative dispute resolution.[42]

81. There are numerous state and federal statutes that mandate alternative dispute resolution or authorize courts to mandate it in particular cases. At the state level, alternative dispute resolution is often mandated to relieve the courts of a large caseload. For example, medical malpractice (Wisconsin Statutes Ann. section 655.43) and family claims (California Family Code section 3170; Delaware Family Court Rule 16) are often subject to mandatory alternative dispute resolution. In addition, alternative dispute resolution is authorized or mandated in various instances. California requires that all lawsuits against the state arising out of public works contracts be submitted to arbitration (California Public Contract Code section 10240). California also requires that civil cases in courts with ten or more judges must be referred to arbitration if the amount in controversy is USD 50,000 or less (Calif. Code of Civil Procedure section 1141.10).

82. In general, there are no state courts of arbitration. Instead, arbitration is conducted by private institutions. Some states have agencies that conduct arbitration in certain cases. For example, the Wisconsin Employment Relations Commission has an arbitration service for employer–employee related disputes.

41. *Arabian American Oil Co. v. Scarfone*, 119 F.R.D. 448 (1988).
42. *Strandell v. Jackson County*, 838 F.2d 884 (1987).

Chapter 4. Obligations of Economic Operators

§1. Corporate Obligations

I. Incorporation

83. The requirements for the incorporation of a legal entity are governed by state law. In general, the basic legal requirement for the incorporation of a legal entity is the filing of articles of incorporation with the Secretary of State. In Delaware, these are referred to as certificates of incorporation. According to Delaware law, the certificate of incorporation must identify the name of the corporation, the address of the registered office, the nature of business, the number of shares of stock the corporation is authorized to issue (and par value), the name and address of the incorporator (§ 102 Delaware General Corporation Law). A legal entity may be incorporated to promote the conduct of any lawful business. Any person or legal entity domestic or foreign may incorporate.

II. Doing Business

84. Once a legal entity is incorporated in one state, it is free to do business throughout the U.S. The other States are required to recognize its existence. However, the states may require the corporation to register as a "foreign corporation" and observe certain other reporting and financial obligations.[43]

85. In order to do business in another state, a corporation must "qualify." The process of qualification is determined by state statute and typically involves the filing of a standard form with the Secretary of State of that jurisdiction. Determining when qualification is necessary is a challenging task. The requirements imposed by each state have been interpreted differently by the courts. A foreign corporation must qualify in that state in order to conduct business there. Failure to qualify can result in the imposition of fines.

III. Annual Reporting

86. All domestic and foreign corporations are generally required to submit an annual report to the Secretary of State of the state where that corporation is registered. The content of the annual report typically covers more detail than the articles of incorporation, that is, the name of the corporation, the address of the registered agent, the names of the officers and directors, the number of shares authorized and

43. The qualification as a foreign corporation in a state other than the state of incorporation does not necessarily give the courts of the "foreign" state general jurisdiction over the foreign corporation. *Genuine Parts Co. v. Cpec*, 2016 WL 1569077 (Del. April 18, 2016).

the amount of the paid-in capital.[44] In the event that the corporation fails to file its annual report, it will be declared "not in good standing" and eventually dissolved ex officio.[45]

§2. Financial Reporting Obligations

87. In addition to federal and state income tax filings, the corporation laws of the various states require payment of taxes or fees upon incorporation as well as annual taxes and fees. Upon incorporation, the state of incorporation will commonly impose a nominal fee. In Delaware for example, this fee is currently USD 89. Similarly, foreign corporations registering to do business in a state are required to pay a registration fee that is often equal to the incorporation fee charged to domestic corporations.

88. A corporation is required to pay income taxes and "franchise" taxes. Income taxes are imposed by both the state and federal governments. Since corporations typically derive revenue from activities in several states, there are rules for allocating income among the states. In addition, corporations (both foreign and domestic) are required to pay a state "franchise" tax for the privilege of doing business in the state. The amount of the franchise tax depends on the particular state statute. Many states use the paid-in capital as the basis for calculating the amount of the annual franchise tax. This franchise tax is not related to franchising in general and is due regardless of whether the corporation is a franchise or not.

44. *See*, e.g., §14.05 Illinois Business Corporation Act.
45. *See*, e.g., §275 Delaware General Corporation Law.

Chapter 5. Business Assets, Goodwill, and Commercial Property Rights

§1. Business Assets

89. The term "business" does not have a uniform meaning in U.S. law. In its broadest sense, the courts have defined it as "any activity engaged in for profit."[46] Its meaning is largely contextual. For example, in the context of the Clayton Act, the term "business" means "an occupation for living or profit, or a commercial or industrial establishment or enterprise."[47] In the context of tax law, a business has been defined simply as "that with which one is busy or occupied."[48]

90. In a general sense, "business assets" include anything that is of value to the business. There are two types of business assets: tangible and intangible. The tangible business assets are the physical objects that are owned by the business such as property, facilities, and equipment. Intangible assets are all other things of value to the company such as goodwill and intellectual property rights. The term "business assets" generally implies ownership of such assets by the business. For example, although the employees of the business are of value to the business, they are not generally considered business assets in the strict sense of the term and are not carried on the balance sheet of the company. Nonetheless, as discussed below, the employees of a business may be part of the company's goodwill.

§2. Goodwill

91. Despite the intangible character of goodwill, it is an important business asset that can be owned and alienated much like tangible property. The U.S. Supreme Court has defined goodwill as every positive advantage that has been acquired by a firm in the progress of its business, whether connected with the premises in which the business was previously carried on, or with the name of the late firm, or with any other matter carrying with it the benefit of the business.[49] The general definition that has been adopted by the courts is the advantage or benefit that is acquired by an establishment, beyond the mere value of its capital stock, funds or property employed therein in consequence of the general public patronage that it receives from repeat customers on account of its position or reputation for skill, efficiency, affluence, punctuality, or even from accidental circumstances.[50] The concept should

46. *State Farm and Casualty Co. v. Geary*, 699 F.Supp. 756, 761 (1987).
47. *Westor Theaters v. Warner Brothers Pictures*, 41 F.Supp. 757, 761 (1941).
48. *Helvering v. Wilmington Trust Co.*, 124 F.2d 156, 158 (1941).
49. *Menendez v. Holt*, 128 U.S. 514, 521 (1888).
50. 38A Corpus Juris Secundum, Goodwill s. 1; *Chance v. Chance*, 694 So. 2d 613, 29, 591 (1997); *Gilmore Ford, Inc. v. Turner*, 599 So. 2d 29, 31(Ala. 1992).

be distinguished from "going concern value" that refers generally to the ability of a business to generate income without interruption even where there has been a change in ownership.[51]

92. Goodwill does not have an independent value. Rather, it is incidental to another aspect of the business. Goodwill can attach not only to a business but also to its management, employees, services, and products. Goodwill, by itself, cannot be transferred and generally would have little value.[52] For example, an owner of a business could not transfer the goodwill associated with a business without selling the business also.

93. Goodwill is a property right protected by law.[53] It may be sold, bequeathed, and damaged. Nonetheless, not all businesses have goodwill. Generally, the business to which it attaches must be profitable.[54] However, a business may have goodwill even if it operates at a loss for a period of time.[55]

94. Just as goodwill is incidental to a business or a part thereof, the goodwill will generally cease to exist when the business to which it is attached ceases to exist.[56] In certain circumstances, however, goodwill has been held to temporarily survive the termination of the business to which it is attached.

95. Goodwill is generally the property of the business. If the business is a stock corporation, a stockholder is the equitable owner of the corporation's goodwill in proportion to the percentage of shares that stockholder holds.[57] This does not mean, however, that the stockholder has the right to transfer the goodwill of the corporation. He can only sell the shares and the goodwill that goes with those shares as evidence of ownership of a corporation that itself has goodwill.

96. Since it is treated as property, goodwill can be transferred by contract or even in testate.[58] The transfer of a business as a going concern implies the transfer of the goodwill of that business unless the parties agree otherwise. If the transfer of a business includes the goodwill, subsequent competition by the transferor of the goodwill will often diminish the value of the goodwill to the transferee. The general

---

51. *Gaydos v. Gaydos*, 693 A. 2d 1368 (1997).
52. *Red Wing Malting Co. v. Willcusts*, 15 F.2d 626 (1926), cert. denied 273 U.S. 763; *Haggin v. Derby*, 229 N.W. 257, 209 (1939).
53. *J.L. Cooper v. Anchor Securities*, 113 P. 2d 845, 849(1941); *Mann v. Fischer*, 51 F.Supp. 550, 551(1943).
54. *Behn v. Shapiro*, 130 N.E. 2d 295 (1955).
55. *Securities Realization Co. v. Peabody & Co.*, 20 N.E. 2d 874 (1939); *Commissioner of Corp. & Taxation v. Ford Motor Co.*, 33 N.E. 2d 318 (1941).
56. *Red Wing Malting Co. v. Willcuts*, 15 F.2d 626 (1926); *Hough Mfg. Corp. v. Virginia Metal Industries, Inc.*, 453 F.Supp. 496 (1978).
57. *First Alabama Bancshares, Inc. v. McGahey*, 355 So. 2d 681 (1977).
58. *Bradbury v. Wells*, 115 N.W. 880 (1908).

rule is that the transferor is not precluded from competing in the absence of a non-compete agreement.[59] However, the transferor can be prevented from intentionally diminishing the value of the goodwill transferred by appealing to the prior customers on the basis of the transferor's prior connection with the business transferred.[60]

§3. Intellectual Property

I. Patents

A. Legislation

97. According to the U.S. Constitution, Congress has the power "to promote the progress of science and useful arts, by securing for limited times to authors and inventors the exclusive right to their respective writings and discoveries" (Article I, section 8). Congress first relied on this authority to enact legislation governing patents in 1790 (Act of April 10, 1790, Chapter 7, 1 Stat. 109). However, the law that is currently in force was enacted in 1952 and is codified in Title 35 of the United States Code. The statutes set forth the requirements of a patent and established the Patent and Trademark Office to administer the law. The federal statute is supplemented by patent regulations codified at Title 37 of the Code of Federal Regulations (C.F.R.). According to the Supreme Court, the purpose of the law is to "promote the progress of science and the useful arts by granting to inventors a limited monopoly that allows them to secure the financial rewards for their inventions."[61]

B. Substantive Requirements

98. In order to be patented, an invention must be patentable, novel, useful and not of an obvious nature.

99. The first requirement is that the invention be of the type that is patentable. According to the law, a patent will be issued only to a process, machine, manufacture, or composition of matter (35 U.S.C. section 101). However, this is not as limiting as it may appear. For example, the term "manufacture" includes "anything under the sun that is made by man."[62] The term "process" refers to a process, act,

59. *Mutual Life Insurance Co. v. Menin*, 115 F.2d 975 (1940) cert. denied 313 U.S. 578; *Warp v. Warp*, 30 N.E. 2d 146 (1940).
60. *Newark Coal Co. v. Spangler*, 34 A. 932 (1896); *Johnson v. Stumbo*, 126 S.W. 2d 165 (1938).
61. *Impression Products, Inc. v. Lexmark Int'l, Inc.*, 137 S.Ct. 1523, 1532 (2017).
62. *Diamond v. Diehr*, 450 U.S. 175 (1981).

or method such as mechanical or technical processes. A "composition of matter" refers to chemical compositions. Abstract ideas, theories, and plans are generally not patentable.[63]

100. An invention must also be novel. An invention is novel if, on the date of filing of the patent application, it was not known or used by others in the U.S. or patented or described in a printed publication in the U.S. or in a foreign country before the invention by the person applying for a patent (35 U.S.C. section 102(a)). An invention is "known by others" if it is accessible to the public.[64] According to some courts, knowledge is "accessible to the public" if there has been no deliberate attempt to keep it secret.[65]

101. A person is not entitled to a patent if the claimed invention was patented, described in a printed publication, or in public use, on sale, or otherwise available to the public before the effective filing date of the claimed invention.

102. The U.S. has now adopted a first to file system. A person is not entitled to a patent if the claimed invention was already described in a patent or in an application for a patent filed before the effective filing date of the claimed invention. (35 U.S.C. section 102(a)).

103. In addition, a patent will be precluded if the invention was patented or described in a printed publication in the U.S. or a foreign country or in public use or on sale in the U.S. more than one year prior to the application for the patent (35 U.S.C. section 102(b)). This latter preclusion is important because it does not depend on when the invention was made. In other words, if the inventor publishes his or her findings or sells the invention, he or she has one year to apply for a patent. If he or she misses this deadline, he or she cannot receive a patent for the invention.

104. A patent may not be granted to an invention unless substantial or practical utility for invention has been discovered and disclosed.[66] General use or commercial of a patented article is evidence of its utility but is not conclusive.[67] However, failure by the assignee of a patent to manufacture and sell a patented device does not negate utility.

105. A patent may not be obtained if the differences between the subject matter sought to be patented and the prior art are such that the subject matter as a whole would have been obvious at the time the invention was made to a person having ordinary skill in the art pertaining to the subject matter. The obviousness of an invention is a legal conclusion involving four factual inquiries, which consist of: (i)

---

63. *Alice Corp. Pty. Ltd. v. CLS Bank Int'l*, 134 S.Ct. 2347 (2014); *Bilski v. Kappos*, 130 S.Ct. 3218 (2010).
64. *Carellav. Starlight Archery*, 804 F.2d 135, 231 USPQ 644 (Fed. Cir. 1986).
65. *W. L. Gore & Assoc. v. Garlock, Inc.*, 721 F.2d 1540, 220 USPQ 303 (Fed. Cir. 1983).
66. *Fujikawa v. Wattenansch*, 93 F.3d 1559 (1996).
67. *Continental Can Co. v. Anchor Hocking Glass Corp.*, 362 F.2d 123 (1966).

the scope and content of prior art; (ii) differences between claims and prior art; (iii) level of ordinary skill in pertinent art; and (iv) secondary considerations.[68]

C. Procedural Requirements

106. Only the inventor may apply for a patent. However, the estate of a deceased inventor or the guardian of an insane or legally incapacitated inventor may apply for patent protection (37 C.F.R. sections 1.42-1.43). It is possible for two or more inventors to apply for a joint patent (37 C.F.R. section 1.45). The general rule is that the nationality of the applicant is irrelevant as to whether the patent application is accepted or rejected.

107. The inventor must submit an application to the Patent and Trademark Office. The application must include a specification of the invention, a drawing, and an oath. It must also be accompanied by a fee. The specification must contain a written description of the invention and of the manner and process of making and using it, in such full, clear, concise, and exact terms as to enable any person skilled in the art to which it pertains, or with which it is most nearly connected, to make and use it. The specification must conclude with one or more claims particularly pointing out and distinctly claiming the subject matter that the applicant regards as the invention. The applicant must also furnish a drawing if necessary for the understanding of the subject matter sought to be patented. If the subject matter necessitates a drawing and the applicant has not furnished one, the Commissioner may require its submission within two months.

108. The applicant must also take an oath that he or she believes himself or herself to be the original and first inventor of the process, machine, manufacture, or composition of matter or improvement for which patent protection is sought. The applicant must also identify the country of which he or she is a citizen. The oath may be made before any person within the U.S. authorized by law to administer oaths, or, when made in a foreign country, before any diplomatic or consular officer of the U.S. authorized to administer oaths.

D. Rights of the Patentee

109. The right granted by the patent is the right to exclude others from making, using or selling the invention in the U.S. or importing the invention into the U.S. In this sense, it is a negative right, that is, the right to exclude others from doing these things. The patent does not specifically grant the inventor the right to do these things himself. The significance of this distinction is that the making, using or selling the invention even by the patent holder must comport with other applicable laws. If, for

68. *Crocs, Inc. v. Commission*, 598 F.3d 1294 (Fed. Cir. 2010); *B.F. Goodrich Co. v. Aircraft Braking Systems Corp.*, 72 F.3d 1577 (1996).

example, the applicable U.S. consumer protection laws prohibit the sale of the patented product, the holder of the patent is precluded from selling that product. This even applies to applicable state law. For example, if a state law requires an inventor a license to sell a particular product, the inventor cannot sell the product without a license even though she may have a patent on the product.

110. One important implication of the negative nature of patent right is that it does not preclude the application of antitrust laws. As discussed below, the federal and state antitrust laws in the U.S. prohibit certain types of conduct that restrain trade. The holding of a patent does not allow the inventor to engage in these practices. In fact, because of the exclusive nature of patents, the holder of a patent may be subject to heightened scrutiny because of his privileged position.

111. The rights that are granted extend only to the geographic territory of the U.S. and its possessions. However, the U.S. is a party to several international conventions relevant to patents. The Paris Convention for the Protection of Intellectual Property codifies the reciprocity principle: each party to the convention agrees to guarantee the same trademark and patent protection to citizens of other countries as it grants to its own citizens. Although there is not a uniform patent in each country, the convention also provides for the right of priority whereby an applicant has a certain period of time to file for patent protection in other countries once he files in one signatory country.[69] The subsequent applications are treated as though they were filed on the same date as the initial application.[70] In other words, the applicant gets "constructive" priority over any applicants who may have filed in the ensuing period.

112. The Patent Cooperation Treaty, to which the U.S. is a party, encompasses over ninety countries. The central objective of this treaty is to facilitate filing procedures in various countries by centralization and harmonization of forms.

113. Patent protection in the U.S. lasts for a period of twenty years from the date on which the application was filed. The term may be extended under certain circumstances. Maintenance fees are due during this period at forty-two months, ninety months, and 138 months. Failure to pay the maintenance fee could lead to the patent being deemed abandoned. Once the patent has expired or been abandoned, anyone else can make, use and sell the invention without having to secure the approval of the inventor. However, they are precluded from receiving a patent on the invention. Even the inventor is precluded once he or she abandons the invention (35 U.S.C. section 102(c)). The patent rights are exhausted upon the first sale of the particular product in the U.S.[71]

---

69. For patents, the time period is twelve months and for trademarks six months.
70. According to U.S. law, the Commissioner of Patents and Trademarks must issue a license before a patent application is made in a foreign country for an invention in the U.S. (37 C.F.R. s. 5.11).
71. *Quanta Computer, Inc. v. LG Electronics*, 553 U.S. 617 (2008); *Fujifilm Corp. v. Benun*, 605 F.3d 1366 (Fed. Cir. 2010).

E. Patent Exhaustion

114. The doctrine of patent exhaustion provides that the initial authorized sale of a patented item terminates all patent rights to that item.[72] The doctrine rests upon the recognition that once a patentee sells an item, it has enjoyed all the rights secured by that limited monopoly.[73] The patentee has bargained for and received full value for the goods.[74] At that point, according to the Supreme Court, "the purpose of the patent law is fulfilled."[75] It does not matter if the first sale occurred in the U.S. or outside the U.S.[76]

F. Inventions by Employees

115. As discussed above, the general rule is that only the inventor may apply for a patent. An employee can file an application for a patent in his own name. The mere fact that he is an employee does not generally give the employer the right to file for the patent. This issue is generally addressed in the employee's contract of employment. Employees who might invent something as part of their employment are often required to enter into an agreement according to which they agree to assign to the employer all inventions made as a result of the employment for the employer. Such restrictions on employees are generally upheld by the courts as long as they are reasonable.[77] Under certain circumstances, such a restriction may even be enforceable if it extends beyond the term of the employment relationship.

116. Absent a specific assignment clause, the unfettered ability of the employee to appropriate inventions that he or she makes at work appears somewhat unfair for the employer at whose expense the invention was probably made. Thus, the courts have recognized what has come to be known as "shop rights."[78] This is an implied nonexclusive license from an employee to an employer to use the patent to which the employee otherwise retains the patent rights. Shop rights in favor of the employer are recognized when the employer shows that the invention was developed by the employee during the employment or with the assistance of the employer's property or labor.

72. *Quanta Computer, Inc. v. LG Electronics, Inc.*, 553 U.S. 617, 625 (2008).
73. *Impression Products, Inc. v. Lexmark Int'l, Inc.*, 137 S.Ct. 1523, 1532 (2017); *Keeler v. Standard Folding Bed Co.*, 15 S.Ct. 738 (1895).
74. *JVC Kenwood Corp. v. Nero, Inc.*, 797 F.3d 1039 (2015); *Keurig, Inc. v. Sturm Foods, Inc.*, 732 F.3d 1370 (D.C.C. 2013).
75. *United States v. Univis Lens Co.*, 62 S.Ct. 1088 (1942).
76. *Impression Products, Inc. v. Lexmark Int'l, Inc.*, 137 S. Ct. 1523, 1533 (2017).
77. *See*, e.g., *Guth v. Minnesota Mining & Mfg. Co*, 72 F.2d 385 (1934).
78. *Schroder v. Tracor*, 217 F.3d 859 (1999).

D. Procedural Requirements

133. Trademarks are protected under common law even if they are not registered.[95] If the owner of the mark would like to register, he or she may do so at either the state or federal level since the U.S. has a dual system of trademark registration. Because it is geographically limited, however, state trademark registration is less common unless it is done in conjunction with federal registration.

134. In order to register a trademark with the U.S. Patent and Trademark Office, the owner of the mark is required to submit an application and pay a filing fee. Once the application is filed, it is examined by an attorney at the U.S. Patent and Trademark Office to determine whether the mark is confusingly similar to another registered mark and whether it is distinctive. Once this determination is made, the mark is published in the Official Gazette of the Patent and Trademark Office. Assuming that no one contests the application in thirty days following the day on which it is published, a certificate of registration is issued by the Patent and Trademark Office. The mark is considered registered for ten years at which time the owner may renew the registration.

E. Rights Conferred by Registration

135. In the U.S., a mark can be registered at the federal and state levels. Once the mark is registered at the federal level, a registrant may give notice that his mark is registered by displaying along with the mark the following words: "Registered in the U.S. Patent and Trademark Office" or "Reg. U.S. Pat. & Tm. Off." or "®" (15 U.S.C. section 1111). The symbol "TM" is used to identify a trademark regardless of whether it is registered or not.

136. The primary benefit of state registration is that it is generally quicker than the federal level. However, if the mark is registered at the state level the protection accorded registration only extends to that state. Therefore, registration is generally done at the federal level. The benefit of registering a mark (as opposed to relying on common law rights) is that it puts third parties on constructive notice of the registrant's claim of ownership over the mark. Registration at the federal level carries with it the added feature that federal courts have jurisdiction over infringement suits and the registrant has certain claims against imports of infringing goods (section 42 Lanham Act). As discussed below, failure to register a mark does not mean that the owner has no rights in relation to third parties who infringe on that mark.

137. Registration of a mark is not necessarily a prerequisite for protection in the U.S. Registration merely carries certain procedural advantages as discussed above. Under the common law, a person who has used a designation as a trademark, trade

95. *Pundzak, Inc. v. Cook, Iowa*, 500 N.W. 2d 424, 430 (1993).

name, collective mark, or certification mark has priority over another user in any geographic area in which that person has used the designation in good faith.[96]

138. Trademark protection under common law endures as long as the trademark remains in use. Registration, however, lasts only ten years but can be renewed if the owner proves that it is still being used. Nonuse for three consecutive years will be prima facie evidence of abandonment. Abandonment is also any course of conduct of the owner, causing the mark to become the generic name for the goods or services on or in connection with which it is used, or otherwise to lose its significance as a mark (15 U.S.C. section 1127).

VI. Copyright

139. In general terms, the term "copyright" refers to the right of an author to control the communication or reproduction of his or her works of authorship fixed in a tangible medium. The right of the federal government in the U.S. to adopt legislation securing copyrights is set forth in the federal Constitution (Article I, section 8, Clause 8). The economic philosophy behind the clause is the conviction that encouragement of individual effort by personal gain is the best way to advance public welfare through the talents of authors and inventors in the sciences and arts.[97] In order to be copyrightable, a work must be considered a work of authorship, it must be in a fixed and tangible medium of expression and it must be original (17 U.S.C. section 102(a)).

A. Substantive Requirements

140. Only certain things qualify as copyrightable subject matter. The common adage is that copyright protects the expression of an idea and not the idea itself. There are eight categories of copyrightable material (17 U.S.C. section 101):

- literary works;
- musical works;
- dramatic works;
- choreographic works;
- pictorial, graphic, and sculptural works;
- motion pictures and audiovisual works;
- sound recordings;
- architectural works.

141. The copyrightable subject matter must be fixed in a form that it can be perceived, reproduced or otherwise communicated. A work is "fixed" in a tangible

96 Restatement Unfair Competition (Third) §19.
97 *Omega S.A. v. Costco Wholesale Corp.*, 776 F.3d 692 (9th Cir. 2015).

medium of expression if it is embodied in a copy or phonorecord, with the permission of the author and is sufficiently permanent or stable to permit it to be perceived, reproduced, or otherwise communicated for a period of more than transitory duration. A work consisting of sounds, images, or both, that are being transmitted, is "fixed" if a fixation of the work is being made simultaneously with its transmission. A performance or a lecture would not qualify for copyright unless they are in a fixed medium.

142. Finally, the work must be original. This is a question of fact that is left up to the courts. However, a copy of an existing work may be copyrightable if it is substantially changed. All work is not copyrightable even if it is substantial. For example, a mere compilation of the names and numbers in the telephone book is not considered to be original.[98] Several categories of materials are generally not eligible for statutory copyright protection. These include, among others: titles, names, short phrases, and slogans, familiar symbols or designs, mere variations or typographical ornamentation, lettering or coloring, mere listings of ingredients or contents.

B. Rights

143. The owner of a copyright has exclusive rights to reproduce the copyrighted work, prepare derivative works based on the copyrighted work and distribute copies of the copyrighted work to the public (17 U.S.C. sections 106(1)–(3)). The owner also has the right to perform or display the copyrighted work publicly (17 U.S.C. sections 106(4)–(5)). For example, the online streaming of a copyright protected performance would constitute copyright infringement.[99] Once the owner of the copyright sells a copy, the copyrights in that copy are exhausted.[100]

144. Traditionally, the author did not have any moral rights in the copyright. When he or she transferred the copyright, he or she lost all rights to control it. However, this changed in 1990 when Congress enacted the Visual Artists Rights Act (VARA) (P.L. 101–650, 104 Stat. 5128, 5132 (December 1, 1990), 17 U.S.C. section 106(A)) as part of the implementation of the Berne Convention. The VARA confers certain attribution and integrity rights to authors of visual or sculptural works and photographs produced for exhibition purposes only. The federal VARA of 1990 grants certain artists the moral rights of attribution and integrity. That is, the author of a work of "visual art" has the right to do the following:

(1) Claim authorship of that work and to prevent the use of his or her name as the author of any work of visual art he or she did not create.

98. *Feist Publications, Inc. v. Rural Telephone Service Co., Inc.*, 499 U.S. 340 (1991).
99. *American Broadcasting Cos. V. Aereo, Inc.*, 134 S.Ct. 2498 (2014).
100. *Kirtsaeng v. John Wiley & Sons*, 113 S. Ct. 1351 (2013); *Vernor v. Autodesk, Inc.*, 621 F.3d 1102 (9th Cir. 2010).

(2) Prevent the use of his or her name as the author of the work in the event of a distortion, mutilation, or other modification of the work that would be prejudicial to his or her honor or reputation.
(3) Prevent any intentional distortion, mutilation, or other modification of that work that would be prejudicial to his or her honor or reputation, and
(4) Prevent any destruction of a work of recognized stature (whether intentional or by gross negligence).

145. The federal copyright laws permit a copyright owner to preclude and recover for any unauthorized copying, that is, infringement, of his or her work. To establish copyright infringement, a copyright holder must show ownership of a valid copyright and unauthorized copying of original, constituent elements of his or her work.[101]

C. Safe Harbor for Internet Service Providers

146. Internet service providers which serve as conduits for copyright infringements may benefit from the protection of a "safe harbor." The four "safe harbors" that limit the liability of Internet service providers for claims of copyright infringement are for (i) transitory digital network communications, (ii) system caching, (iii) information residing on systems or networks at the direction of users, and (iv) information location tools.[102] The threshold requirements are as follows: (1) the party must be a "service provider" as that term is defined by the statute; (2) the party must have adopted and reasonably implemented a policy for termination of repeat infringers; and (3) the party must not interfere with standard technical measures used by copyright owners to identify or protect copyrighted works.[103] There is no affirmative duty on the Internet service provider to proactively search for and prevent copyright infringements.[104]

D. Duration

147. Whereas trademark protection begins with use, copyright protection begins upon creation of the work. A work is "created" when it is fixed in a copy or phonorecord for the first time. If a work is prepared over a period of time, the portion of it that has been fixed at any particular time constitutes the work as of that time. Copyright protection lasts for the life of the author plus fifty years (17 U.S.C. section 302(a)). In the event that the copyrighted work was for hire, the protection lasts until the earlier of seventy-five years from publication or 100 years from creation.

101. *Aaberg v. Francesca's Collections, Inc.*, 2018 WL 1583037 (Mar. 27, 2018) S.D.N.Y).
102. 17 U.S.C. § 512(a)-(d).
103. *Viacom Int'l, Inc. v. YouTube, Inc.*, 676 F.3d 19 (2d Cir. 2012); *Capitol Records LLC v. Vimeo LLC*, 972 F.Supp.2d 537 (S.D.N.Y. 2013).
104. *Viacom Int'l, Inc. v. YouTube, Inc.*, 676 F.3d 19, 41 (2d Cir. 2012).

with predetermined patterns, intended to perform electronic circuitry functions. A "mask work" is a series of related images representing the predetermined, three-dimensional pattern or metallic, insulating, or semiconductor material of a semiconductor chip product. A mask work is "fixed" in a semiconductor chip product when its embodiment in the product is sufficiently permanent or stable to permit the mask work to be perceived or reproduced from the product for a period of more than transitory duration.

161. A mask work fixed in a semiconductor chip product, by or under the authority of the owner of the mask work, is eligible for protection if on the date on which the mask work is registered, or is first commercially exploited anywhere in the world, the owner of the mask work is: (i) a national or domiciliary of the U.S.; (ii) a national, domiciliary, or sovereign authority of a foreign nation that is a party to a treaty affording protection to mask works to which the U.S. is also a party; or (iii) a stateless person, wherever that person may be domiciled.

162. Protection is not available for mask work that is not original or consists of designs that are staple, commonplace, or familiar in the semiconductor industry, or variations of such designs, combined in a way that, considered as a whole, is not original. In no case does the protection for a mask work extend to any idea, procedure, process, system, method of operation, concept, principle, or discovery, regardless of the form in which it is described, explained, illustrated, or embodied in such work.

163. The owner of a mask work has the exclusive rights to reproduce the mask work and to import or distribute a semiconductor chip product in which the mask work is embodied (17 U.S.C. section 905). The exclusive rights in a mask work belong to the owner of the mask work. The owner may transfer all of those rights, or license all or less than all of those rights, by any written instrument signed by such owner or a duly authorized agent of the owner. Such rights may be transferred or licensed by operation of law, may be bequeathed by will, and may pass as personal property by the applicable laws of intestate succession (17 U.S.C. section 903(b)).

164. The owner of a mask work may apply to the Register of Copyrights for registration of a claim of protection in a mask work. However, the application for registration of a claim of protection in the mask work must be made within two years after the date on which the work is first commercially exploited anywhere in the world. The protection provided to a mask work ends ten years after the date on which such protection commences (17 U.S.C. section 904).

§9. Trade Secret

165. Trade secrets are protected under both federal and state law. There is no uniform definition of what constitutes a "trade secret." According to the Federal Defend Trade Secrets Act and the Economic Espionage Act, a "trade secret" is defined as all forms and types of financial, business, scientific, technical, economic, or engineering information, including patterns, plans, compilations, program devices, formulas, designs, prototypes, methods, techniques, processes, procedures, programs, or codes, whether tangible or intangible, and whether or how stored, compiled, or memorialized physically, electronically, graphically, photographically.[123] Under state law, the term "trade secret" includes any information or compilation of information that is closely held and used in one's business and that gives its owner advantage over the competition who do not know it.[124]

One unique characteristic of a trade secret—as opposed to other forms of intellectual property—is that it is not limited in time. It is generally protected as long as it is kept secret.

166. Matters of public knowledge cannot qualify as trade secrets.[125] There is no uniform list of factors to consider when deciding whether information constitutes a trade secret. Common considerations include: (1) the extent to which the information is known outside the business of the entity claiming the trade secret, (2) the extent to which it was known by employees and others involved in the business, (3) the extent of the measures taken by the entity to guard the secrecy of the information, (4) the value of the information to the entity and its competitors, (5) the amount of effort or money expended by the entity in developing the information, and (6) the ease or difficulty with which the information could be properly acquired or duplicated by others.[126] When information can be derived from research, there must be at least a fair degree of inconvenient or difficult research required before information will be accorded status as "trade secret."[127]

Under federal law, the owner of a trade secret that is misappropriated may bring a civil action if the trade secret is related to a product or service used in, or intended for use in, interstate or foreign commerce.[128] State trade secret laws, which are not preempted by the federal legislation, also provide for civil claims for misappropriations of trade secrets. All states (with the exception of Massachusetts and New York) have adopted the Uniform Trade Secrets Act (UTSA).

In order to succeed on a claim for misappropriation of trade secrets, a plaintiff must demonstrate: (1) the existence and ownership of a trade secret, (2) the breach of a confidential relationship or improper discovery of a trade secret, (3) use or disclosure of a trade secret, and (4) damages to the owner.[129] Some factors that the

123. Defend Trade Secrets Act, Public Law No: 114-153 (May 11, 2016); Economic Espionage Act of 1996, Pub.L. 104–294, Oct. 11, 1996, 110 Stat. 3488, 18 USCA §§ 1831 to 1839.

124. *Rodgard Corp. v. Miner Enterprises, Inc.*, 914 F.Supp. 907, 923 (1995); *Geritrec Corp. v. Dermarite Industries, LLC*, 910 F.Supp. 955, 961 (1996).

125. Conversely, information does not qualify as a trade secret merely because it is not publicly known. *Weins v. Sporleder*, 569 N.W. 2d 16 (1997).

126. *Heil Trailer Int'l Co. v. Kula*, 542 Fed.Appx. 329 (5th Cir. Oct. 16, 2013); *Astoria Indus. of Iowa, Inc. v. SNF, Inc.*, 223 S.W.3d 616, 634-35 (Tex. App. 2007); *Sands v. Estate of Buys*, 160 S.W.3d 684, 687-88 (Tex. App. 2005).

127. *Amoco Production Co. v. Laird, Inc.*, 622 N.E. 2d 912, 918 (1993).

128. Defend Trade Secrets Act, Public Law No: 114-153 (May 11, 2016).

129. *Heil Trailer Int'l Co. v. Kula*, 542 Fed.Appx. 329 (5th Cir. Oct. 16, 2013); *Cuidado Casero Home Health of El Paso, Inc. v. Ayuda Home Health Care Servs., LLC*, 404 S.W.3d 737, 744 (Tex. App. 2013); *Bohnsack v. Varco, L.P.*, 668 F.3d 262, 279 (5th Cir. 2012).

court may consider in determining whether information qualifies as a "trade secret" include the extent to which information is known outside the owner's business, the extent to which it is known by employees and others involved in the owner's business, the extent of measures taken by the owner to guard the secrecy of the information, value of information to the owner and to his competitors, the amount of effort or money expended by the owner in developing information, and the ease or difficulty with which information could be properly acquired or duplicated by others.[130]

130. *Christopher M's Hand Poured Fudge, Inc. v. Hennon*, 699 A. 2d 1272 (1997).

Chapter 6. Bankruptcy and Related Institutions

§1. Sources of Bankruptcy Law

167. Under the English common law, debtors who were unable to pay their debts were subject to imprisonment. The U.S. Bankruptcy Act of 1841 extended certain protection to debtors and was the first statute in the U.S. to address bankruptcy issues.[131] Currently, the Banking Reform Act of 1978, as amended, forms the foundation for U.S. bankruptcy law (11 U.S.C. sections 101 et seq. (often referred to as the "Bankruptcy Code")). The authority of the federal government to legislate in this area is granted by the federal Constitution (U.S. Constitution Article I. section 8). The federal bankruptcy laws preempt state law in this area if they regulate the same issue.[132]

§2. Objectives of Bankruptcy Law

168. In general terms, U.S. bankruptcy law has two objectives. One is to afford the honest debtor with a "fresh start." The other is to ensure a degree of fairness of distribution of assets among the creditors.

§3. Jurisdiction in Bankruptcy Cases

169. In the U.S. legal system, most courts have general subject matter jurisdiction. That is, they can hear different types of claims ranging from criminal to contract cases. One exception to this is bankruptcy law. According to the Bankruptcy Amendments and Federal Judgeship Act of 1984, the federal district courts have jurisdiction over bankruptcy cases (28 U.S.C. section 151). Within the federal district courts, there are special bankruptcy courts to which bankruptcy cases are referred.

§4. Venue

170. A bankruptcy case may be commenced in the federal district court in which the domicile, residence, principal place of business in the U.S., or principal assets in the U.S. of the person or entity that is the subject of such case have been located for 180 days immediately preceding such commencement (28 U.S.C. section 1408(1)).

---

131. Charles J. Tabb, *The History of the Bankruptcy Laws in the United States*, 3 *ABI L. Rev.*, 5 (1995).
132. *Sturges v. Crowninshield*, 17 U.S. (4 Wheat.) 122 (1819).

§5. Types of Bankruptcy Protection

171. In the U.S., there are two types of bankruptcy: liquidation and reorganization (Chapters 11 through 13 of the Bankruptcy Code). The vast majority of bankruptcy cases in the U.S. are liquidations under Chapter 7 of the Bankruptcy Code.

172. Generally, any individual or legal entity may file for bankruptcy protection under the Bankruptcy Code (11 U.S.C. section 101(41)). However, the Bankruptcy Code prevents railroads, insurance companies, and banks from filing for bankruptcy protection (11 U.S.C. section 109). A foreign debtor may file for bankruptcy protection in the U.S. if it resides or has a domicile, a place of business or property in the U.S. (11 U.S.C. section 109).

§6. Chapter 7 Bankruptcies

173. A typical Chapter 7 (liquidation) case has five stages: commencement, collection, liquidation, distribution, and discharge. The first stage is the commencement of the case by filing a petition of bankruptcy with the bankruptcy court. Although the creditors may, under certain circumstances, file the petition (involuntary bankruptcy), in the vast majority of cases it is the debtor who files the bankruptcy petition under Chapter 7 (voluntary bankruptcy) (11 U.S.C. section 301).

174. The filing of the bankruptcy creates what is referred to as the "property of the estate" (i.e., all of the property of the debtor at the time of the filing). The second stage is the collection of the property of the estate by the bankruptcy trustee. This includes any property that the debtor may have transferred prior to filing for bankruptcy protection. The bankruptcy trustee is not an employee of the state. Instead, he or she is appointed by the court and is compensated for his or her work (11 U.S.C. section 326). In the alternative, the creditors may agree on a trustee.

175. The third stage is the liquidation of the property of the estate. Since all distributions to the creditors are in cash, the property collected by the bankruptcy trustee must first be liquidated and then distributed. At the distribution stage, one must distinguish between secured and unsecured creditors. Secured creditors will receive the proceeds from the sale of the property in which they have a security interest. As for unsecured creditors, they receive pro rata distributions of the proceeds of the liquidation. Security interests are discussed below in greater detail.

176. In making distributions of the proceeds of the liquidation, certain claims have priority status (11 U.S.C. section 507). For example, the administrative expenses and unsecured claims for contributions to an employee benefit plan are given priority.

177. Similarly, unsecured claims of individuals, to the extent of USD 1,950 for each such individual, are also given priority if they arose from the deposit, before the commencement of the case, of money in connection with the purchase, lease, or rental of property for the personal, family, or household use of such individual.

178. The final stage in the Chapter 7 proceedings is the discharge of the debtor from any liability for its debts created prior to the filing for bankruptcy protection. Under certain circumstances, however, the debtor will not be discharged (11 U.S.C. section 727(1)). If the debtor has intentionally hindered, delayed, or defrauded a creditor, the debt will not be discharged.

§7. Chapters 11 & 13 Bankruptcies

179. Another type of bankruptcy is the reorganization under Chapters 11 through 13 of the Bankruptcy Code. In contrast to a Chapter 7 bankruptcy, however, the debtor in a Chapter 13 bankruptcy retains his or her property and prepares a plan proposing payments to creditors. The property remains with the debtor. Instead of satisfying the creditors from the liquidation of the property of the estate, the creditors in a Chapter 13 case typically receive funds from the ongoing operations of the debtor in accordance with a plan. In other words, Chapter 13 is designed to rehabilitate the debtor.

180. Chapter 13 proceedings begin in much the same way as Chapter 7 proceedings. The first step is the filing of a bankruptcy petition with the court. The U.S. trustee then appoints a bankruptcy trustee (11 U.S.C. section 1302(a)). Another basic difference is that only creditors are eligible to file a petition under Chapter 13 (11 U.S.C. section 301). In other words, there is no "involuntary" bankruptcy under Chapter 13.

181. The next step is the proposal of a plan by the debtor to the creditors. The court then reviews the plan and confirms or rejects it. If the debtor fails to timely file a plan, the court may convert the filing to a Chapter 7 case (11 U.S.C. section 1307(c)(3)). The Bankruptcy Code identifies the requirements of the plan (11 U.S.C. section 1322(a)). The plan must provide for the submission of all or such portion of future earnings or other future income of the debtor to the supervision and control of the trustee as is necessary for the execution of the plan. In addition, the plan must provide for the full payment, in deferred cash payments, of all claims entitled to priority, unless the holder of a particular claim agrees to a different treatment.

182. Although a creditor may object to the plan (11 U.S.C. section 1324), it is up to the court to confirm it. The court will confirm the plan if it has been proposed in good faith and not by any means forbidden by law (11 U.S.C. section 1325). In addition, the value of property, as of the effective date of the plan, to be distributed under the plan on account of each allowed unsecured claim must not be less than the amount that would be paid on such claim if the estate of the debtor were liquidated under Chapter 7. With respect to each allowed secured claim provided for by the plan, the holder of such claim must have accepted the plan. Finally, the court must be convinced that the debtor will be able to make all payments under the plan and to comply with the plan.

183. If the trustee or the holder of an allowed unsecured claim objects to the confirmation of the plan, then the court may not approve the plan unless the value of the property to be distributed under the plan on account of such claim is not less than the amount of such claim; or the plan provides that all of the debtor's projected disposable income[133] to be received in the three-year period beginning on the date that the first payment is due under the plan will be applied to make payments under the plan.

184. Once the court has confirmed the plan, it is binding on the debtor and the creditors (11 U.S.C. 1327(a)). The debtor must make the payments called for by the plan and the court may order any entity from which the debtor receives income to pay all or any part of such income to the trustee. Once he or she does so, he or she is discharged from the debt (11 U.S.C. 1328(a)). In contrast to a Chapter 7 filing, the only types of debts that are not discharged are claims for alimony and child support and any claims identified in the plan.

§8. Chapter 9 Bankruptcies

185. Under Chapter 9 of the Bankruptcy Code, a municipality may file for bankruptcy protection against its creditors. Although these types of bankruptcies are relatively rare, they tend to attract a significant amount of media attention. A municipality may only file under Chapter 9 if it has been authorized to do so under state law. The proceedings are commenced in much the same way as a Chapter 7 case, that is, by filing a petition for relief. The court, and not the trustee, has exclusive authority to supervise the reorganization of the municipality's debt.

I. Automatic Stay

186. Once the bankruptcy petition is filed, it operates as a stay of litigation against the debtor (11 U.S.C. section 362). The stay includes enforcement proceedings of a judgment obtained before the commencement of the case, any act to obtain possession of property of the estate and any act to collect, assess, or recover a claim against the debtor that arose before the commencement of the case.

133. The term "disposable income" means income which is received by the debtor and which is not reasonably necessary to be expended for the maintenance or support of the debtor or a dependent of the debtor and the payment of expenditures necessary for the continuation, preservation, and operation of such business.

II. Avoidance Actions

A. Preferences (Section 547 Bankruptcy Code)

187. Even transactions occurring before the filing of the bankruptcy petition may be challenged. The bankruptcy trustee may avoid any transfer of an interest of the debtor in property to or for the benefit of a creditor, for or on account of an antecedent debt owed by the debtor before such transfer was made; made while the debtor was insolvent; or made on or within ninety days before the date of the filing of the petition (11 U.S.C. section 547(b)). The trustee may not avoid a transfer to the extent that such transfer was intended by the debtor and the creditor to or for whose benefit such transfer was made to be a contemporaneous exchange for new value given to the debtor, or to the extent that such transfer was in payment of a debt incurred by the debtor in the ordinary course of business or financial affairs of the debtor and the transferee.

B. Fraudulent Conveyances

188. There are certain types of conveyances that will be avoided by the bankruptcy trustee because they are deemed to be "fraudulent." A conveyance may be considered fraudulent if, within one year prior to the date on which the bankruptcy petition was filed, the debtor made a transfer with actual intent to hinder, delay, or defraud any present or future creditor (11 U.S.C. section 548(a)(1)). The trustee may also avoid a transfer if the debtor received less than a reasonably equivalent value in exchange and was insolvent or became insolvent as a result, was engaged in business, or a transaction, or was about to engage in business or a transaction, for which any property remaining was an unreasonably small capital; or intended to incur, or believed that the debtor would incur, debts that would be beyond the debtor's ability to pay as such debts matured (11 U.S.C. section 548(a)(2)).

III. Debtor's Discharge

189. The essential component of U.S. bankruptcy is the discharge of the debtor from its pre-petition. The bankruptcy court will grant the debtor a discharge of its debts unless the debtor has engaged in fraud or has transferred, removed, destroyed, mutilated, or concealed property of the debtor within one year before the date of the filing of the petition (11 U.S.C. section 727). The discharge discharges the debtor from all debts that arose before the date of the order for relief. On request of a party in interest, the court may order the trustee to examine the acts and conduct of the debtor to determine whether a ground exists for denial of discharge.

§9. ALTERNATIVES TO BANKRUPTCY

I. Composition Agreements

190. Bankruptcy proceedings are often lengthy and impose significant costs on the parties. When a debtor is faced with the inability to pay all of its debts, it is often more advantageous for all parties concerned to reach an agreement among themselves without filing a bankruptcy proceeding. A "composition agreement" refers to an agreement between a debtor and two or more of its creditors by which the creditors agree to receive a portion of their debt in full satisfaction of their claims.

191. A specific form is not required to give effect to the composition agreement. The basic requirement is that the debtor and two or more creditors are party to the agreement. An agreement between a debtor and only one of its creditors is not considered a composition agreement. A composition agreement between a debtor's creditors (without the agreement of the debtor) does not amount to an effective composition agreement even if it includes all of that debtor's creditors. In most instances, however, the creditors only give their assent under the condition that all other creditors agree to the composition.

192. In order to be considered an effective composition, there must be a meeting of the minds between the debtor and the creditors. Consequently, unilateral promises are not effective and binding as compositions. This often arises where the creditors agree among themselves to an allocation of assets and then present the plan to the debtor. In such circumstances, the composition is not effective until it is accepted by the debtor. Whether mutuality exists is a question of fact to be determined in each case.

193. No extrinsic consideration is required for an effective composition agreement. The consideration for the agreement lies in the consent of the creditors to accept part of a debt in satisfaction of the whole.[134] The debtor receives relief from the debt, and the creditors receive a secure payment. The alternative in most cases would be for the debtor to seek protection from its creditors in bankruptcy.

II. Assignment for the Benefit of Creditors

194. One alternative to bankruptcy is the assignment for the benefit of creditors. This practice, which is sometimes referred to as a voluntary assignment, has the benefit of avoiding the costs associated with a formal bankruptcy filing.

195. In contrast to composition agreements, this alternative is based on the concept of a trust. It involves the transfer of assets by the debtor to an agreed-upon

134. *Union Central Life Ins. Co. v. Weber*, 2 N.E.2d 746 (1936).

assignee who then holds the assets in trust for the benefit of the creditors. The trustee is generally instructed to liquidate the assets and distribute the proceeds to the creditors.

196. The assignment for the benefit of creditors is effective only on those creditors who consented to the assignment. A creditor may implicitly consent by accepting a distribution. Since the assignment for the benefit of creditors involves a transfer of title to the assets, the nonconsenting creditors cannot reach the assets. They are left with the option of forcing an involuntary bankruptcy or challenging the assignment as a fraudulent transfer.

III. Bulk Sales Laws

197. In order to protect creditors from the "secret" sales of a debtor's assets or a substantial portion of assets, many states have enacted "bulk sales laws" that are based on Article 6 of the UCC. The bulk sales laws are designed to prevent debtors from putting their assets beyond the reach of their creditors. The law of the state where the assets are located applies.

198. Bulk sale means a sale not in the ordinary course of the seller's business of more than half the seller's inventory if on that date the buyer has notice, or after reasonable inquiry would have had notice, that the seller will not continue to operate the same or a similar kind of business after the sale (UCC section 6-102). The amount of the assets being sold as a proportion of the debtor's overall assets is generally used to determine whether the assets being transferred are substantial.[135] Sales of assets with a value of less than USD 10,000 are exempted (UCC section 6-103(3)). In addition, the bulk sales laws typically do not apply to the following types of transfer:

(i) a transfer made to secure payment or performance of an obligation;
(ii) a transfer of collateral to a secured party;
(iii) a sale of an asset encumbered by a security interest or lien if:
  - all the proceeds of the sale are applied in partial or total satisfaction of the debt secured by the security interest or lien; or
  - the security interest or lien is enforceable against the assets after it has been sold to the buyer and the net contract price is zero;
(iv) a general assignment for the benefit of creditors or to a subsequent transfer by the assignee;
(v) a sale by an executor, administrator, receiver, trustee in bankruptcy, or any public officer under judicial process; or
(vi) a sale made in the course of judicial or administrative proceedings for the dissolution or reorganization of an organization.

135. *Key Capital Corp. v. M&S Liquidating Corp.*, 542 N.E.2d 603 (1989).

In addition, if the buyer has its principal place of business in the U.S., the bulk sales laws will not apply if the buyer assumes in full the debts that were incurred in the seller's business before the date of the bulk sale, is not insolvent after the assumption and gives written notice of the assumption not later than 30 days after the date of the bulk sale by sending or delivering a notice to each creditor whose debt is assumed or by filing a notice in the office of the Secretary of State.

199. The bulk sales laws apply to companies engaged in the sale of goods. Companies exclusively engaged in the sale of services do not generally fall under the bulk sales laws.[136]

200. In order to protect the creditors of the seller, the bulk sales law requires that the debtor notifies its creditors when it makes a bulk transfer of its assets. The transferor must supply the transferee with a schedule of property and a list of creditors. The buyer then gives constructive notice to the creditors by making a public filing of the transfer.

201. A buyer who fails to comply with the bulk sales law requirements with respect to a creditor is liable to the creditor for damages in the amount of the claim, reduced by any amount that the creditor would not have realized if the buyer had complied (UCC section 6-107(1)).

136. *Professional Marketing Distributors, Inc. v. Feldman Associates, Inc.*, 414 S.E.2d 666 (1991).

Chapter 7. Secured Transactions

202. A secured transaction generally refers to an agreement that grants a creditor a security interest in specific assets of the debtor. Such transactions are governed by Article 9 of the UCC. The creation of a security interest requires: (1) a security agreement, (2) value given by the secured party, and (3) debtor rights in the collateral (UCC section 9-203(1)). The security agreement must indicate an intent of the parties to create a security interest and contain a description of the collateral.

203. A debtor is not generally prohibited from granting multiple security interests in the same asset. This often leads to competing claims between secured parties in the event of default by the debtor. The process by which a secured party acquires preference over other secured parties is called perfection. The creation of the security interest relates to the relationship between the creditor and the debtor. Perfection concerns the relationship between multiple creditors.

204. Perfection serves the purpose of publicizing the fact that the creditor holds a secured interest in the assets (i.e., that the assets are encumbered). Once the secured interest is perfected, it has priority over subsequent secured interests. An unperfected security interest has little value. Such security interests are subordinate to the rights of perfected security interests.

205. There are few ways to perfect a security interest: filing, possession, control, and automatic perfection. The most common method is to file a financing statement (UCC section 9-302(1)). This is a standard form that needs to be filled out and filed with the local public register. In most states, this is done at the county level. Failure to file in the proper office may mean that the security interest is not perfected.[137] However, a financing statement must not be filed to perfect a security interest in collateral in possession of the secured party or a purchase money security interest in consumer goods or a security interest in a deposit account. If a secured party assigns a perfected security interest, no filing is required in order to continue the perfected status of the security interest against creditors of and transferees from the original debtor.

206. Another common method to perfect a security interest is simply to take possession of the collateral (UCC section 9-302(1)(a)). The fact that the secured party has possession of the asset serves as notice to the third parties that the assets are encumbered. However, certain types of collateral cannot be perfected by possession such as a security interest in the rights to proceeds of a written letter of credit. Such rights can be perfected only by the secured party's taking possession of the letter of credit. A security interest in money or instruments (other than instruments that constitute part of chattel paper) can be perfected only by the secured party's taking possession.

137. *In re Value Investment Properties, LLC*, 481 B.R. 403 (Bankr. E.D. Tenn. 2012).

the instrument, including any right as a holder in due course. However, the transferee cannot acquire rights of a holder in due course by a transfer from a holder in due course if the transferee engaged in fraud or illegality affecting the instrument (UCC section 3-203). Unless otherwise agreed, if an instrument is transferred for value and the transferee does not become a holder because of lack of endorsement by the transferor, the transferee has a specifically enforceable right to the unqualified endorsement of the transferor. In such cases, however, negotiation of the instrument does not occur until the endorsement is made.

§8. Endorsement

223. The concept of endorsement is important to the law of negotiable instruments because it often determines the holder in due course. It refers to a signature, other than that of the maker or drawer that alone or accompanied by other words is made on an instrument for the purpose of: (1) negotiating the instrument; (2) restricting payment of the instrument; or (3) incurring endorser's liability on the instrument. If an instrument is payable to a holder under a name that is not the name of the holder, endorsement may be made by the holder in the name stated in the instrument or in the holder's name or both, but signature in both names may be required by a person paying or taking the instrument for value or collection.

224. There are three types of endorsement: special endorsement; blank endorsement; anomalous endorsement. A special endorsement is an endorsement made by the holder of an instrument, whether payable to an identified person or payable to bearer, and the endorsement identifies a person to whom it makes the instrument payable. When specially endorsed, an instrument becomes payable to the identified person and may be negotiated only by the endorsement of that person (UCC section 3-206).

225. If an endorsement is made by the holder of an instrument and it is not a special endorsement, it is a "blank endorsement." When endorsed in blank, an instrument becomes payable to bearer and may be negotiated by transfer of possession alone until specially endorsed. The third type of endorsement, the "anomalous endorsement," is an endorsement made by a person that is not the holder of the instrument. An anomalous endorsement does not affect the manner in which the instrument may be negotiated (UCC section 3-206).

226. A restrictive endorsement is an endorsement limiting payment to a particular person or otherwise prohibiting further transfer or negotiation of the instrument. An endorsement stating a condition to the right of the endorsee to receive payment does not affect the right of the endorsee to enforce the instrument. A person paying the instrument or taking it for value or collection may disregard the condition, and the rights and liabilities of that person are not affected by whether the condition has been fulfilled.

Chapter 9. Documents of Title

227. The term "document of title" generally refers to documents that, in the regular course of business or financing, are treated as adequately evidencing that the person in possession of it is entitled to receive, hold and dispose of the document and the goods it covers (UCC section 7-104). Examples of documents of title are bills of lading, dock warrants, dock receipts, and warehouse receipts for the delivery of goods. The most common form of document of title used in commercial transactions is the bill of lading. This is a document evidencing the receipt of goods for shipment issued by a person engaged in the business of transporting or forwarding goods and includes an airbill.

228. To be a document of title, a document must purport to be issued by or addressed to a bailee and purport to cover goods in the bailee's possession that are either identified or are fungible portions of an identified mass (UCC section 1-201(15)). A document of title is negotiable if the goods are to be delivered to bearer or to the order of a named person (UCC section 7-104).

229. A holder to whom a negotiable document of title has been duly negotiated acquires title to the document and to the goods and all rights accruing under the law of agency or estoppel, including rights to goods delivered to the bailee after the document was issued.

230. A negotiable document of title made to the order of a named person is negotiated by his endorsement and delivery. After endorsement in blank or to bearer, any person can negotiate it by delivery alone. A negotiable document of title is also negotiated by delivery alone when by its original terms it runs to bearer. When a document running to the order of a named person is delivered to him, the effect is the same as if the document had been negotiated.

Chapter 10. Letters of Credit

§1. Definition

231. Similar to negotiable instruments, letters of credit are governed by state law. They are not governed by common law contract principles because they evolved as a part of the law of merchants. Article 5 of the UCC applies to letters of credit. The following analysis is based on the UCC provisions. The term "letter of credit" refers to a definite authenticated undertaking by an issuer to a beneficiary at the request or for the account of an applicant or, in the case of a financial institution, to itself or for its own account, to honor a documentary presentation by payment or delivery of an item of value (UCC section 5-102).

§2. Independence Principle

232. There are typically three parties involved in the issuance of a letter of credit: the applicant, the issuer, and the beneficiary. The "applicant" is the person at whose request or for whose account a letter of credit is issued. The bank or the other person that issues a letter of credit is referred to as the "issuer." The "beneficiary" is the person who under the terms of a letter of credit is entitled to have its complying presentation honored. Each of the three relationships created by these different roles is independent of the others. This is known as the independence principle.[139] This means that the rights and obligations of an issuer to a beneficiary or a nominated person under a letter of credit are independent of the existence, performance, or nonperformance of a contract or arrangement out of which the letter of credit arises or that underlies it, including contracts or arrangements between the issuer and the applicant and between the applicant and the beneficiary (UCC section 5-104).

§3. Issuance of the Letter of Credit

233. A letter of credit is issued and becomes enforceable according to its terms against the issuer when the issuer sends or otherwise transmits it to the person requested or to the beneficiary. The general rule is that a letter of credit is irrevocable unless it expressly states that it is revocable. If there is no stated expiration date or other provision that determines its duration, a letter of credit expires one year after the date on which it is issued.

---

139. In re Circuit City Stores, Inc. 2016 WL 1714515 (E.D. Va. April 26, 2016); Gerald T. McLaughlin, *Exploring Boundaries: A Legal and Structural Analysis of the Independence Principle of Letter of Credit Law*, 119 Banking L.J. 501 (2002).

§4. Honoring the Letter of Credit

234. Upon timely presentation of the conforming documents specified in the letter of credit, the issuer has an obligation to honor the letter of credit. The issuer has the obligation to examine the documents to determine whether they comply with the terms of the letter of credit. There are two standards used by the courts to assess conformity. The standard of "strict compliance" requires that the terms and conditions of the letter of credit are strictly observed.[140] The alternative standard adhered to by a minority of jurisdictions is "substantial compliance." According to this standard, the courts require strict compliance in determining whether the beneficiary was entitled to honor the letter of credit but allow for substantial compliance in determining whether the issuer is entitled to reimbursement from the applicant after the issuer has honored the letter of credit.[141]

§5. Transfer of Letters of Credit

235. The right of a beneficiary to draw or otherwise demand performance under a letter of credit may not be transferred unless the letter of credit provides for its transfer (UCC section 5-112). However, even if a letter of credit provides that it is transferable, the issuer may refuse to recognize or carry out a transfer if the transfer would violate applicable law. This does not, however, prevent the beneficiary from assigning the proceeds of a letter of credit.

140. *BasicNet S.p.A. v. CFP Services Ltd.*, 127 A.D.3d 157 (N.Y. 2015); Imptex *Intern. Corp. v. HSBC Bank USA*, N.A. 52 A.D.3d 215 (N.Y. 2008).
141. *Bank of Cochin v. Manufacturers Hanover Trust*, 612 F.Supp. 1533 (1985).

Chapter 11. Commercial Contracts

§1. General Principles of Contract Law

236. The general principles of contract law in the U.S. are based in the common law. The American Law Institute, a private institution in the U.S., attempted in 1932 to set forth the general principles of contract law in the Restatement of Contracts. This is largely an attempt to bring some order to the common law rules that are sometimes conflicting and difficult to decipher. The current edition, the (Second) Restatement of Contracts, was adopted in 1979. The Restatement is an authoritative source of law, but not binding.

§2. Uniform Commercial Code

237. The significance of the common law of contracts and the restatement has been diminished as far as the sale of goods is concerned because of the widespread adoption of the UCC. Because of the federal structure of the U.S. legal system, there were efforts in the late 1800s to attempt to adopt uniform laws that would serve to promote convergence between the different states and federal jurisdictions. In 1892, NCCUSL was convened to undertake this task.

238. By 1906, the NCCUSL had approved a Uniform Sales Act that was applicable to the sale of goods. During the ensuing forty-six years, thirty-seven states adopted the Uniform Sales Act. In 1951, the NCCUSL approved the first version of the UCC to replace the Uniform Sales Act. Article 2 of the UCC applies to the sale of goods. It has been adopted by all states except Louisiana. Hence, the law applicable to the sale of goods in the U.S. is largely statutory law. Nonetheless, the common law continues to apply to the extent that the provisions of the UCC do not address a particular situation. In addition, reference to case law is often essential to understanding the meaning of the UCC provisions. The following discussion relating to the sale of goods is based primarily on Article 2 of the UCC.

Chapter 12. Sale of Goods

§1. Formation

I. Offer and Acceptance

239. The common law rule is that a contract is formed when one party makes an offer that the other party accepts. The UCC, however, allows for the creation of a contract "in any manner sufficient to show agreement, including conduct by both parties which recognizes the existence of a contract" (UCC section 2-204(1)).[142] Acceptance may occur in any manner and by any medium reasonable in the circumstances unless the offer states otherwise. An order or other offers to buy goods for prompt or current shipment is considered as inviting acceptance either by a prompt promise to ship or by the prompt shipment of the goods.

240. In the event that a purported acceptance states terms additional to or different from those offered, it is considered by the UCC as an acceptance unless it is expressly made conditional on assent to the additional or different terms. However, the additional or different terms do not become a part of the contract. Instead, they are to be construed as proposals for addition to the contract. Between merchants, however, such terms do become part of the contract unless the offer expressly limits acceptance to the terms of the offer or they materially alter it.

II. Formal Requirements

241. A contract for sale of goods may be made in any manner sufficient to show agreement. Even though one or more terms are left open a contract for sale does not fail for indefiniteness if the parties have intended to make a contract and there is a reasonably certain basis for giving an appropriate remedy.[143] A contract may exist even though the price for the goods is still open (UCC section 2-305(1)). In such a case, the price is a "reasonable price" at the time for delivery.[144] If, however, the contract is clear that it is not binding until a price is agreed upon, then there is no contract.

Generally, a writing is not required for an agreement to be enforceable. A contract for the sale of goods may be made in any manner sufficient to show agreement, including conduct by both parties that recognize the existence of such a contract. The UCC, however, requires that a contract for the sale of goods for the price of USD 500 or more be in writing (UCC section 2-201). However, a contract

142. Article 2 of the UCC only applies to the sale of "goods." The sale of investment securities, for example, would not be governed by Art. 2 of the UCC. *Lehman Bros. Holdings, Inc. v. Nat'l Bank of Arkansas*, 875 F.Supp. 2d 911 (E.D. Ark. 2012). If a contract covers both goods and services, the predominant purpose test is applied. *Warschaw v. QBE Ins. Corp.*, 2012 WL 3648453 (D. Mass. Aug. 22, 2012).

143. *Dell's Maraschino Cherries Co. v. Shoreline Fruit Growers, Inc.*, 887 F.Supp. 2d 459 (E.D.N.Y. 2012).

144. *Sae Biang Optical v. Kenmark Optical, Inc.*, 489 F. App'x 826 (6th Cir. 2012).

which does not satisfy this requirement may be enforceable if the goods are to be specially manufactured for the buyer and are not suitable for sale to others in the ordinary course of the seller's business.[145]

§2. Performance

242. The obligation of the seller under the UCC is to transfer and deliver the goods. The obligation of the buyer is to accept the goods and pay in accordance with the contract. Unless the parties have agreed otherwise, all goods must be tendered in a single delivery. The place for delivery of goods is the seller's place of business unless the parties agreed otherwise. The time for shipment or delivery or any other action under a contract, if not agreed upon, is a reasonable time.

243. Tender of payment is sufficient when made by any means or in any manner current in the ordinary course of business. In order to be valid, tender of payment on a contract must be: (1) timely; (2) made to the person entitled to payment; (3) unconditional; (4) an offer to pay the amount of money due; and (5) coupled with an actual production of the money or its equivalent.[146] A payment is considered tendered when it is mailed, not when it is received.[147]

§3. Delegation and Assignment

244. A party to a contract for the sale of goods may delegate his or her duties unless otherwise agreed or unless the other party has a substantial interest in having his original promisor perform or control the acts required by the contract (UCC section 2210). However, the delegation of performance does not relieve the delegating party of any duty to perform or any liability for breach. Similarly, all rights of either seller or buyer can be assigned except where the assignment would materially change the duty of the other party, increase materially the burden or risk imposed on him by his contract, or materially impair his chance of obtaining return performance. A prohibition of assignment of the contract is to be construed as barring only the delegation to the assignee of the assignor's performance. An assignment of the contract or of "all my rights under the contract" or an assignment in similar general terms is an assignment of rights and, unless the language or the circumstances (as in an assignment for security) indicate the contrary, it is a delegation of performance of the duties of the assignor.

145. *Atlas Container Corp. v. H&W Corrugated Parts, Inc.*, 2012 WL 3240434 (D. Md. Aug. 2, 2012).
146. *Brady v. Park*, 302 P.3d 1220 (Utah 2013).
147. *Procacci v. Procacci*, 729 So.2d 522, 523 (Fla. 1999).

§4. WARRANTIES

245. There are two types of warranties: implied and express. Implied warranties are those that are included in each sale regardless of whether the vendor has actually made the particular representation to the buyer. Express warranties are those that have expressly been made by the vendor.

I. Implied Warranties

246. The three implied warranties imposed by the UCC are the warranty of merchantability, the warranty of fitness for a particular purpose and the warranty of title. The warranty of merchantability is implied in a contract if the seller is a merchant with respect to goods of that kind. Merchantability means that the goods pass without objection in the trade under the contract description and are fit for the ordinary purposes for which such goods are used, are adequately contained, packaged, and labeled as the agreement may require, and conform to the promises or affirmations of fact made on the container or label if any. The warranty of fitness for particular purpose means that the goods shall be fit for the particular purpose for which the goods are being acquired if the seller, at the time of contracting, has a reason to know any particular purpose for which the goods are required and that the buyer is relying on the seller's skill or judgment to select or furnish suitable goods. Finally, there is an implied warranty of title. This means that the seller of goods automatically warrants that the goods will be delivered free from any security interest or other lien or encumbrance of which the buyer at the time of contracting has no knowledge.

II. Express Warranties

247. An express warranty is one that is created by the conduct of the seller. For example, any affirmation of fact or promise made by the seller to the buyer that relates to the goods and becomes part of the basis of the bargain creates an express warranty that the goods conform to the affirmation or promise. Any description of the goods that is made part of the basis of the bargain creates an express warranty that the goods shall conform to the description. Any sample or model that is made part of the basis of the bargain creates an express warranty that the whole of the goods conforms to the sample or model.

III. Limitation of Warranties

248. Both implied and express warranties can be limited. To exclude or modify the implied warranty of merchantability, the language in the contract must mention merchantability and must be conspicuous. To exclude or modify any implied warranty of fitness, the exclusion must be by a writing and conspicuous. Language to exclude all implied warranties of fitness is sufficient if it states, for example, that

"There are no warranties which extend beyond the description on the face hereof." Unless the circumstances indicate otherwise, all implied warranties are excluded by expressions like "as is," "with all faults," or other language that, in common understanding, calls the buyer's attention to the exclusion of warranties and makes plain that there is no implied warranty.

§5. Delivery of Goods

249. For delivery, the UCC requires that the seller put and hold conforming goods at the buyer's disposition and give the buyer any notification reasonably necessary to enable him or her to take delivery. Delivery must be at a reasonable hour. The seller has the duty to keep the goods available for the period reasonably necessary to enable the buyer to take possession. Where goods are in the possession of a bailee, and are to be delivered without being moved, delivery is affected by delivering of a negotiable document of title covering such goods.

250. Where the seller is required or authorized to send the goods to the buyer, and the contract does not require him to deliver them at a particular destination, the seller must put the goods in the possession of such a carrier and make such a contract for their transportation as may be reasonable having regard to the nature of the goods and other circumstances of the case. In addition, the seller must obtain and promptly deliver or tender in due form any document necessary to enable the buyer to obtain possession of the goods or otherwise required by the agreement or by usage of trade and promptly notify the buyer of the shipment.

251. The UCC relies on delivery terms similar to INCOTERMS. According to the designation Free On Board (FOB) at the place of shipment, the seller must deliver the goods to that place and bear the expense and risk of putting them into the possession of the carrier. If the term FOB is the place of destination, the seller must at his or her own expense and risk, transport the goods to that place and tender delivery of them.

252. The term "free alongside ship" at a named port means that the seller must at his own expense and risk deliver the goods alongside the vessel in the manner usual in that port or on a dock designated and provided by the buyer. In addition, the seller is required to obtain and tender a receipt for the goods in exchange for which the carrier is under a duty to issue a bill of lading.

253. The term Cost, Insurance, Freight (CIF) means that the price includes the cost of the goods and the insurance and freight to the named destination. The term C&F or CF means that the price includes cost and freight to the named destination. The term CIF destination or its equivalent requires the seller at his own expense and risk to put the goods into the possession of a carrier at the port for shipment and obtain a negotiable bill of lading covering the entire transportation to the named destination. It also requires the seller to load the goods and obtain a receipt from the carrier (which may be contained in the bill of lading) showing that the freight has been paid or provided for and obtain a policy or certificate of insurance. The term C&F or its equivalent has the same effect and imposes upon the seller the same obligations and risks as a CIF term except the obligation as to insurance. Under the term CIF or C&F, unless otherwise agreed; the buyer must make payment against tender of the required documents and the seller may not tender nor the buyer demand delivery of the goods in substitution for the documents.

§6. Inspection

254. Unless otherwise agreed, the buyer of goods has a right before payment or acceptance to inspect the goods at any reasonable place and time and in any reasonable manner (UCC section 2-512). When the seller is required or authorized to send the goods to the buyer, the inspection may be after their arrival. The expenses associated with the inspection must be borne by the buyer but may be recovered from the seller if the goods do not conform to the contract and are rejected.

§7. Risk of Loss

255. In the absence of breach of contract by either party, the risk of loss passes to the buyer when the goods are delivered to the carrier if the contract requires or authorizes the seller to ship the goods by carrier (UCC section 2-509). If, however, the contract specifically allocates the risk of loss to one of the parties, then that party bears the risk of loss. If the goods fail to conform to the contract, the risk of their loss remains on the seller until cure or acceptance.

Part II. Economic Law

Chapter 1. General Principles

§1. Principles of Economic Law

I. Fundamental Rights of Those Engaged in Economic Activities

256. Laws effectively limit the activities of certain classes of individuals or legal entities. In the U.S. legal system, legislation appropriately adopted by the federal government is generally deemed to reflect the will of the people. The rights of individuals and legal entities such as businesses are inferior to federal laws unless such rights are enumerated in the U.S. Constitution. In other words, an individual or business cannot contest a law adopted by the federal government unless that law infringes on a constitutional right held by such individual or business.

257. Whether a fundamental right extends to a particular person or entity depends on the particular right as enumerated in the Constitution. Generally, fundamental rights found in the U.S. Constitution apply to all natural persons. Some of these rights are even extended to aliens within the territory of the U.S. Corporations in the U.S. enjoy some constitutional rights such as property rights.

258. The U.S. Constitution enumerates certain rights that are protected against encroachment by any level of government, that is, federal, state or local. In addition, many statutes grant certain rights. The difference is that a right granted by statute can generally be encroached upon, restricted or even withdrawn by the government that granted the right. In general, rights are granted to specific subjects, for example, persons.

259. The concept of "person" generally applies to both legal and natural persons.[148] Whether a certain provision of the Constitution or a particular statute applies specifically to legal entities depends on the intent of the particular provision on statute. In interpreting statutes to determine whether the concept "person" includes legal entities, the decisive question is the intent of the legislator to include legal entities.

---

148. *Klein v. Board of Tax Supervisors*, 282 U.S. 19 (1930); *McKinely v. Wheeler*, 130 U.S. 630 (1889).

260. Another common subject of laws is citizens. For jurisdictional purposes, a legal entity is considered a citizen in that state in which it is organized.[149] As to the issue of substantive rights, however, a legal entity is not considered a "citizen" unless the purpose of the particular constitutional provision or statute suggests otherwise.[150] For example, the provision of the U.S. Constitution that accords "citizens" of one state all the privileges and immunities of the citizens of other states (Article 4 section 2, U.S. Constitution) does not apply to corporations.[151]

261. Another common category for purposes of government regulation is "businesses affected with a public interest." This is a term that must be defined in each case as the Supreme Court has refused to provide an exact definition.[152] A legal entity is not affected with a public interest merely on the basis of its size.[153] Instead, its existence must benefit the public good beyond merely the benefits that arise from providing a good or service for a certain price, for example, a public utility. The significance of the distinction is that businesses affected with the public interest have an obligation to act reasonably with the public.[154] Accordingly, the states' authority to regulate such businesses is greater.

II. Property Rights

262. The U.S. Constitution guarantees certain properties to persons. According to the Fifth Amendment, no "person" shall be deprived of property without due process of law. The Fourteenth Amendment requires the states to respect this right as regards persons within the jurisdiction of that state. The Supreme Court has repeatedly held that this right extends to legal entities.[155] This right includes the right to operate a business or pursue an occupation. A person's business and occupation are considered to be "property" for purposes of the property rights accorded by the Constitution.[156] The right includes the right to enter into contracts in furtherance of such occupation or business.[157]

§2. Freedom of Contract

263. The notion of freedom of contract not only serves as a basis of the U.S. economic system but is also guaranteed by the U.S. Constitution. It is also a

149. *Doctor v. Harrington*, 196 U.S. 579 (1905).
150. *See*, e.g., *Sioux Falls Taxpayers Association v. Sioux Falls*, 7 N.W. 2d 136 (1942).
151. *Asbury Hospital v. Cass County*, 326 U.S. 207 (1945); *Hemphill v. Orloff*, 277 U.S. 537 (1928).
152. *Ribnik v. McBride*, 277 U.S. 350 (1928).
153. *Williams v. Standard Oil Co. of Louisiana*, 278 U.S. 235 (1929).
154. *Wolff Packing Co. v. Court of Industrial Relations of Kansas*, 262 U.S. 522 (1923).
155. *First National Bank v. Bellotti*, 435 U.S. 765 (1978); *Grosjean v. American Press Co.*, 297 U.S. 233 (1936); *Pierce v. Society of Sisters*, 268 U.S. 510 (1925).
156. *Terrace v. Thompson*, 263 U.S. 197 (1923); *Gosney v. Sonora Independent School Dist.*, 603 F. 2d 522 (1979).
157. *Chicago R.I. v. US*, 284 U.S. 80 (1931).

fundamental right protected by many state constitutions. This freedom exists as a corollary to the rights to liberty and property that are expressly enumerated in the Constitution. Accordingly, it is extended to commercial legal entities[158] Freedom of contract is not absolute. It is subject to reasonable legislative regulation.[159] Although a statute may legitimately derogate from the freedom of contract, such statute must be strictly construed.[160]

§3. Association

264. The freedom of association is not specifically and expressly addressed by the U.S. Constitution. Nonetheless, the Supreme Court has held that such a constitutional right exists as a corollary to the freedom of speech that is secured by the First Amendment.[161] Although the freedom of association has been asserted in the context of political speech, it also extends to the situation where individuals associate to pursue economic interests.[162] However, protection is accorded to an economic association only if the economic activities are sufficiently expressive to invoke the freedom of speech.[163] In other words, the freedom of association does not exist as an independent right.

§4. Regulation of Business Activities

265. The rights extended to legal persons are not absolute. The government can regulate business activities if such regulation is necessary to protect public health, morals, and welfare of the people. This applies to the right to property,[164] the freedom of contract,[165] the freedom of association and the freedom to pursue an occupation or trade.[166] Although none of these rights are absolute in the absence of a genuine threat to the public, regulation of the conduct is prohibited if it encroaches upon one of these rights.[167]

---

158. *Mellon Bank v. Aetna Business Credit, Inc.*, 619 F. 2d 1001 (1980).
159. *Schmidinger v. Chicago*, 226 U.S. 578 (1913); *Daniel Loughran Co. v. Lord Baltimore Candy & Tobacco Co.*, 12 A.2d 201, 204 (1940).
160. *New England Mutual Life Insurance Co. v. Mitchell*, 118 F.2d 414 (1941); *A&M Pest Control Service, Inc. v. LaBurre*, 170 So.2d 855 (1965).
161. *Coates v. City of Cincinnati*, 402 U.S. 611 (1971)
162. *United Transp. Union v. State Bar of Michigan*, 40 U.S. 576 (1971); *Griswold v. Connecticut*, 381 U.S. 479 (1965).
163. *FTC v. Superior Court Trial Lawyers Ass'n.*, 493 U.S. 411 (1990).
164. *National Fertilizer Ass'n. v. Bradley* 301 U.S. 178 (1937).
165. *Midwest Messenger Ass'n. v. Spire*, 393 N.W. 2d 438 (1986).
166. *Eye Dog Foundation v. State Board of Guide Dogs*, 432 P. 2d 717 (1967).
167. *Citizens United v. Federal Election Commission*, 558 U.S. 310 (2010).

§5. Means of Regulation

266. Although the state may legitimately regulate certain business conduct, its authority is not unlimited. The means of regulation must have a reasonable relationship to the objective that justifies the encroachment, that is, protection of public health, safety, and welfare.[168] The regulation of the business conduct may exist in the form of a prohibition of such conduct.[169] In such cases, however, there must not be another reasonable mode of regulation that is less restrictive. This is similar to the proportionality standard common in Europe. It is a factual issue to be decided in each case. The reasonableness of the regulation will depend, in part, on the nature of the business. For example, regulation of "business affected with a public purpose" is generally more reasonable than the same regulation as applied to other businesses.[170]

267. The state may also regulate the terms and conditions of business conduct provided that such regulation is necessary to protect the public. For example, the state may require that a particular business obtain a permit or license prior to engaging in certain conduct that poses a threat to the public. Such regulation, although it limits the rights of the business, may be justified. Similarly, the state may regulate the qualifications required to engage in a particular business or occupation.[171]

268. The state may also legitimately regulate the time and place of business conduct.[172] Here again, the state is subject to the requirement that such regulation is necessary to protect the public. For example, laws regulating the hours in which a business could open have been held unconstitutional because the connection with the protection of public welfare was too tenuous.[173]

§6. Price Regulation

269. As discussed above, the U.S. Constitution protects the freedom to contract and to pursue a business or occupation. Laws that regulate the price at which individuals sell or buy goods or services encroach upon these rights. Yet, there are numerous laws that regulate prices. Where the effect on price is merely incidental to an otherwise legitimate law, the effect will not generally be sufficient to make the law unconstitutional.[174] However, the authority of the state to set or directly regulate prices must be justified as a protection of the public welfare.[175] The price regulation must be incidental to a policy that the state has the authority to adopt. The arbitrary regulation of prices independent of a legitimate policy objective violates

168. *Church v. State*, 646 N.E. 2d 572 (1995).
169. *Great Atlantic & Pacific Tea Co. v. Grosjean*, 301 U.S. 412 (1937).
170. *State v. Spears*, 259 P. 2d 356 (1953).
171. *Semler v. Oregon State Board of Dental Examiners*, 294 U.S. 608 (1935).
172. *Reinman v. City of Little Rock*, 237 U.S. 171 (1915).
173. *Olds v. Klotz*, 3 N.E. 2d 371 (1936).
174. *Nebbia v. People of New York*, 291 U.S. 502 (1934).
175. *Id.*

the Constitution.[176] The regulation of prices is legitimate, for example, when the state is protecting consumers from monopoly pricing practices by dominant businesses,[177] or to prevent the charging of unreasonable rent to tenants in a situation of a shortage of housing.[178]

176. *Pennell v. City of San Jose*, 485 U.S. 1 (1988).
177. *FCC v. Florida Power Corp.*, 480 U.S. 245 (1987).
178. *Pennell v. City of San Jose*, 485 U.S. 1 (1988).

Chapter 2. Regulation of Commercial Activities

§1. Regulation of Banking Activities

I. National Banks

270. The banking regulatory regime in the U.S. distinguishes between national banks and state banks. In general terms, national banks are federally chartered and active in more than one state. The primary source of authorities of national banks is the National Bank Act (12 U.S.C. sections 1 et seq.) and regulations promulgated under that authority by the Office of the Comptroller of Currency. They are identified by the words "national" or "national association," or the initials "N.A." in the title of the bank. A "state bank" is any bank, banking association, trust company, savings bank, industrial bank, or other banking institution that is engaged in the business of receiving deposits (other than trust funds) and is incorporated under the laws of any state.

271. A national bank may deal in, underwrite, purchase, and sell securities for its own account as limited by the Comptroller of the Currency (12 C.F.R. section 1.3). Federally chartered banks are only subject to state laws of general application in their daily business to the extent such laws do not conflict with the National Bank Act. For example, state usury laws govern the maximum rate of interest national banks can charge on loans, and state contract laws govern national bank contracts. Federal preemption also applies to wholly-owned state-chartered operating subsidiary of a national bank was subject to federal regulation.[179]

272. There are several public agencies responsible for the interpretation and application of the regulations applicable to banks. At the federal level, the Comptroller of the Currency is the administrative agency responsible for interpreting the National Bank Act. Other federal agencies are the Federal Deposit Insurance Corporation, the Board of Governors of the Federal Reserve System (responsible for the Bank Holding Company Act), the Office of Thrift Supervision (responsible for the Home Owners Loan Act), and the Federal Trade Commission (FTC) (with consumer protection and competition related regulatory authority). At the state level, each state has its own regulatory regime and oversight.

273. In order to become active as a national bank, the entity must file articles of association and an organization certificate. Upon filing, the national bank has the authority to make contracts, to sue and be sued, complain and defend, in any court of law and equity, as fully as natural persons, to elect or appoint directors and officers, adopt bylaws regulating the manner in which its stock shall be transferred, its directors elected or appointed, its officers appointed, its property transferred, its general business conducted, and the privileges granted to it by law exercised and

179. *Watters v. Wachovia Bank*, 550 U.S. 1 (2007).

enjoyed and to exercise "all such incidental powers as shall be necessary to carry on the business of banking" (12 U.S.C. section 24).

274. The task of defining the concept "business of banking" has been left up to the Comptroller of the Currency and the courts. For example, national banks have been deemed to have the authority to sell credit-related insurance[180] and to broker variable and fixed annuity contracts.[181] Recent changes to the law have allowed national banks to sell title insurance in states that permit state banks to do so.

II. State Banks

275. State banks are regulated by the respective "state bank supervisor" in the state in which they are chartered. In addition, its authorities and limits on its activities are defined by state law. Because each state will have slightly different regulations and interpretations, a discussion of the various state regulatory regimes is omitted.

276. It should be noted, however, that federal regulations are also relevant to the activities of state banks. Under the Federal Deposit Insurance Corporation Improvement Act, a state bank may not engage as principal (as opposed to an agent) in any type of activity that is not permissible for a national bank unless the Federal Deposit Insurance Corporation has determined that the activity would pose no significant risk to the appropriate deposit insurance fund. In addition, the state bank must comply with applicable capital standards prescribed by the appropriate federal banking agency (12 U.S.C. section 1831a). State banks are prohibited by federal law from engaging in insurance underwriting and from acquiring or retaining any minority equity investment except to the extent that such activity is permissible for national banks under federal law.

III. Bank Holding Companies

277. There is separate federal legislation applicable to bank holding companies. These are any companies that own, control, or have the power to vote 25% or more of any class of voting securities of any bank or bank holding company, or that control in any manner the election of a majority of the directors of any bank or bank holding company, or that the Federal Reserve Board determines, after notice and opportunity for a hearing, control directly or indirectly the management or policies of any bank or bank holding company. The applicable law is the Bank Holding Company Act (12 U.S.C. sections 1841 et seq.). The fundamental purpose of the

180. *Independent Brokers Ass'n of Am. v. Heimann*, 613 F.2d 1164 (1979).
181. *Nations Bank of North Carolina v. Variable Annuity Life Insurance Company*, 513 U.S. 251 (1995).

bank holding company legislation is to prevent the possibility that a holding company would abuse its control over commercial bank credit for the benefit of its non-banking operations.

278. Under the Bank Holding Company Act (12 U.S.C. sections 1841 et seq.), any company wishing to obtain control or ownership of a bank, or any bank wishing to place itself under the control or ownership of another company, must first obtain approval of the Federal Reserve Board.[182] The act excludes several classes of institutions from its definition of "bank." For example, foreign banks with a U.S. branch are expressly excluded (12 U.S.C. section 1841(c)(2)(A)), as are institutions that do not do business within the U.S. except as an incident to activities outside the U.S. (12 U.S.C. section 1841(c)(2)(C)).

279. The Bank Holding Company Act prohibits the Federal Reserve Board from approving any acquisition, merger, or consolidation that would result in a monopoly, or that would be in furtherance of any combination or conspiracy to monopolize or to attempt to monopolize the business of banking in any part of the U.S. It also prohibits any acquisition, merger or consolidation the effect of which may be to substantially lessen competition, or to tend to create a monopoly, unless it finds that the anticompetitive effects of the proposed transaction are clearly outweighed in the public interest by the probable effect of the transaction in meeting the convenience and needs of the community to be served (12 U.S.C. section 1842(c)).

IV. Savings and Loan Holding Companies

280. The Financial Institution Reform, Recovery, and Enforcement Act of 1989 (12 U.S.C. section 1467a) applies to savings and loan holding companies. The term savings and loan holding company is defined as any company that directly or indirectly controls a savings association or controls any other company that is a savings and loan holding company (12 U.S.C. section 1467a(a)(1)(D)(i)). A person is deemed to have control of a savings association if the person directly or indirectly, or with others, or through subsidiaries, owns, controls, or holds power to vote more than 25% of the voting shares of the association, or controls the election of a majority of the association directors (12 U.S.C. section 1467a(a)(2)(A).

281. Within ninety days after becoming a savings and loan holding company, the company must register with the Director of the Office of Thrift Supervision. It is required to submit information with respect to the financial condition, ownership, operations, management, and intercompany relationships of such holding company and its subsidiaries (12 U.S.C. section 1467a).

182. *Whitney Nat'l Bank v. Bank of New Orleans & Trust Co.*, 379 U.S. 411.

V. Regulation of International Banking Activities

282. Federal law allows any national banking association possessing a capital and surplus of USD 1,000,000 or more to file an application with the Board of Governors of the Federal Reserve System for permission to establish branches in foreign countries for the furtherance of the foreign commerce of the U.S. (12 U.S.C. section 601). In addition, any national banking association may apply to the Board of Governors to acquire and hold, directly or indirectly, stock or other evidence of ownership in one or more banks organized under the law of a foreign country and not engaged, directly or indirectly, in any activity in the U.S. However, before any national bank is permitted to purchase stock, the bank must enter into an agreement with the Board of Governors of the Federal Reserve System to restrict its operations or conduct its business in such manner or under such limitations and restrictions as the said board may prescribe. The Board of Governors of the Federal Reserve System may require such national banks to dispose of stock holdings in the bank upon reasonable notice if it fails to comply with the regulations (12 U.S.C. section 603).

283. Corporations to be organized for the purpose of engaging in international or foreign banking or other international or foreign financial operations, either directly or through the agency, ownership, or control of local institutions in foreign countries, may be formed by any number of natural persons greater than four (12 U.S.C. section 611). Such a corporation must have a capital stock of at least USD 2,000,000, one-quarter of which must be paid in before the corporation may be authorized to begin business. The remainder of the capital stock must be paid in installments (12 U.S.C. section 618).

284. A majority of the shares of the capital stock of corporations engaged in international or foreign banking must at all times be held and owned by citizens of the U.S. or by firms or companies, the controlling interest in which is owned by citizens of the U.S. (12 U.S.C. section 619).

§2. Regulation of Exchanges

I. Securities Exchanges

285. In the U.S., the term "security" is defined broadly. It encompasses any note, stock, treasury stock, bond, debenture, evidence of indebtedness, certificate of interest or participation in any profit-sharing agreement, collateral trust certificate, preorganization certificate or subscription, transferable share, investment contract, voting-trust certificate, certificate of deposit for a security, fractional undivided interest in oil, gas, or other mineral rights, any put, call, straddle, option, or privilege on any security, certificate of deposit, or group or index of securities (including any interest therein or based on the value thereof) (15 U.S.C. section 77a). The regulation of the securities markets takes a bifurcated approach. On the one hand, there are the federal securities laws (i.e., the Securities Act of 1933 and the Securities

Exchange Act of 1934). On the other hand, these federal laws are augmented by the rules and regulations of the securities exchanges themselves that are largely self-regulating bodies.

286. In general terms, the Securities Act of 1933 regulates the sale of securities while the Securities Exchange Act of 1934 regulates the functioning of the exchanges. The general rule is that in order to be able to effect any transaction in a security or to report any such transaction, the exchange must be registered as national securities exchange (15 U.S.C. section 78e).

287. The Securities and Exchange Commission (SEC) is the primary body charged with the enforcement of the federal securities laws. The SEC is comprised of five Commissioners who are appointed by the President each appointed for five-year terms. A maximum of three Commissioners can be members of the same political party. Registration of an exchange is affected by filing the appropriate form with the SEC, an application for registration. The SEC then has to determine whether the exchange is properly organized and has the capacity to comply and to enforce compliance by its members and persons associated with its members with the applicable laws and the rules of the exchange.

288. In order to be sold on an exchange, a security must be registered. In order to register a security, the issuer must file the appropriate application with the exchange (the SEC only receives a copy) (15 U.S.C. section 78e). All persons utilizing exchange facilities to effect transactions involving securities (other than an exempted security or commercial paper, bankers' acceptances, or commercial bills) must be registered (15 U.S.C. section 780). A securities broker or dealer may be registered by filing with the SEC an application for registration.

289. In abstract terms, "exchange" means any organization, association, or group of persons, whether incorporated or unincorporated, which constitutes, maintains, or provides a market place or facilities for bringing together purchasers and sellers of securities (15 U.S.C. section 781). There are two primary securities exchanges in the U.S.: the New York Stock Exchange and the American Stock Exchange. Similar to stock exchanges throughout the world, these exchanges serve as clearinghouses for the sale of securities that they list. In addition to these two national securities exchanges, there are seven regional exchanges located in Boston (Boston Stock Exchange), Chicago (Chicago Board Options Exchange), Cincinnati (Cincinnati Stock Exchange), Intermountain Stock Exchange, Midwest Stock Exchange, Pacific Stock Exchange, and Philadelphia (Philadelphia Stock Exchange).

II. Insider Trading

290. The federal securities laws make it unlawful for any person directly or indirectly, by the use of any means or instrumentality of interstate commerce, or of the mails or of any facility of any national securities exchange, to employ any device, scheme, or artifice to defraud, to make any untrue statement of a material fact or to omit to state a material fact necessary in order to make the statements made, in the light of the circumstances under which they were made, not misleading, or to engage in any act, practice, or course of business that operates or would operate as a fraud or deceit upon any person in connection with the purchase or sale of any security (15 U.S.C. section 78t-1). These practices are considered insider trading.

291. In cases of insider trading, the SEC has the authority to bring an action in a U.S. federal district court to seek a civil penalty to be paid by the person who committed such violation. The SEC may also bring an action to seek a civil penalty to be paid by a person who, at the time of the violation, directly or indirectly controlled the person who committed such violation. The amount of the penalty may not exceed three times the profit gained or loss avoided as a result of the insider trading. In addition, a penalty up to the greater of USD 1,000,000, or three times the amount of the profit gained or loss avoided as a result of such controlled person's violation can be imposed on any person who, at the time of the violation, directly or indirectly controlled the person who committed such violation.

III. Regulation of Investment Advisers

292. In contrast to brokers and dealers of securities, there are no self-regulatory organizations similar to the National Association of Securities Dealers that regulate investment advisers.[183] An "investment adviser," in contrast to a broker or a dealer, is a person who, for compensation, engages in the business of advising others, either directly or through publications or writings, as to the value of securities or as to the advisability of investing in, purchasing, or selling securities, or who, for compensation and as part of a regular business, issues or promulgates analyzes or reports concerning securities. It does not include, however, any lawyer, accountant, engineer, or teacher whose performance of such services is solely incidental to the practice of his or her profession.

293. Since investment advisers only provide advice and do not actually sell the security, regulation is somewhat more relaxed. The primary legislation is the Investment Advisers Act. To the extent that an investment adviser manages investment company assets or pension plan assets, the Investment Company Act and the Employee Retirement Income Security Act come into play. Similar to brokers and dealers, investment advisers are required to register with the SEC or the states in

183. A "broker" means any person engaged in the business of effecting transactions in securities for the account of others, but does not include a bank. "Dealer" means any person regularly engaged in the business of buying and selling securities for his own account, through a broker or otherwise, but does not include a bank, insurance company, or investment company, or any person insofar as he is engaged in investing, reinvesting or trading in securities, or in owning or holding securities, for his own account, either individually or in some fiduciary capacity, but not as a part of a regular business.

which they are active. Once registered, investment advisers have the affirmative duty to provide certain information to their clients. In addition, the Act prohibits certain conduct by the investment adviser.

IV. Commodities Exchanges

294. The Commodity Exchange Act (7 U.S.C. section 1) makes it unlawful for any person to offer to enter into or to conduct any office or business anywhere in the U.S. for the purpose of dealing in any transaction in connection with a contract for the purchase or sale of a commodity for future delivery unless such transaction is conducted on or subject to the rules of a board of trade that has been designated by the Commodity Futures Trading Commission (CFTC) as a "contract market" for such commodity. "Commodity" is defined as certain "enumerated commodities"[184] and "all other goods and articles ... and all services, rights, and interests in which contracts for future delivery are presently or in the future dealt in." (7 U.S.C. section 1(a)(4)).

295. The primary regulatory entity is the CFTC, which is composed of five Commissioners appointed by the President. The CFTC has the authority of designating the boards of trade as a contract market. The term "board of trade" means any exchange or association of persons who are engaged in the business of buying or selling any commodity or receiving a commodity for sale on consignment.

296. These exchanges are private entities. They all perform self-regulatory functions in order to maintain their status as contract markets. Most of the exchanges are owned by their members. The one prominent exception is the New York Futures Exchange, which is owned by the New York Stock Exchange. The organization and operation of the exchanges are regulated by internal bylaws adopted by the respective exchanges. They all have internal governing boards and committees charged with supervising the conduct of its members. Access to the respective trading floors is determined by the internal rules of the particular exchange.

§3. Regulation of Foreign Investment and Trade

I. National Security

297. The Omnibus Trade and Competitiveness Act of 1988 introduced the "Exon-Florio provision" into the Defense Production Act of 1950 (50 U.S.C. App. section 2170) which was subsequently amended by the Foreign Investment Risk

184. The "enumerated commodities" are wheat, cotton, rice, corn, oats, barley, rye, flaxseed, grain sorghums, mill feeds, butter, eggs, *Solanum tuberosum* (Irish potatoes), wool, wool tops, fats and oils (including lard, tallow, cottonseed oil, peanut oil, soybean oil, and all other fats and oils), cottonseed meal, cottonseed, peanuts, soybeans, soybean meal, livestock, livestock products, and frozen concentrated orange juice.

Review Modernization Act of 2018. The Exon-Florio provision (as amended) grants the President of the U.S. the authority to review and suspend or prohibit any merger, acquisition, joint venture, or takeover by or with any foreign person that could result in foreign control of any U.S. business. It also covers "foreign government-controlled transactions" and transactions involving "critical infrastructure" and "critical technologies." A foreign government-controlled transaction means any covered transaction that could result in the control of any person engaged in interstate commerce in the U.S. by a foreign government or an entity controlled by or acting on behalf of a foreign government. Critical infrastructure means systems and assets, whether physical or virtual, so vital to the U.S. that the incapacity or destruction of such systems or assets would have a debilitating impact on national security. Critical technologies means defense articles or defense services included on the United States Munitions List, items included on the Commerce Control List (CCL), chemical and biological weapons proliferation, nuclear nonproliferation, or missile technology or specially designed and prepared nuclear equipment, parts and components, materials, software and technology, nuclear facilities, equipment and material, select agents and toxins, and emerging and foundational technologies (50 U.S.C. App. section 2170(a)).

298. The law is administered by the Committee on Foreign Investment in the United States (CFIUS). The CFIUS spans several agencies within the Executive Branch. The Secretary of the Treasury serves as the chairperson of the Committee. The other members are the heads of the Department of Justice (DOJ), the Department of Homeland Security, the Department of Commerce, the Department of Defense, the Department of State, the Department of Energy, the Office of the U.S. Trade Representative, and the Office of Science & Technology Policy. The Director of the National Intelligence and the Secretary of Labor are nonvoting members of CFIUS. The Secretary of the Treasury designates, as appropriate, a member or members of the Committee to be the lead agency or agencies on behalf of the Committee for each covered transaction (50 U.S.C. App. section 2170(k)).

299. The President, acting through the Committee, may review any covered transaction to determine the effects of the transaction on the national security of the U.S. Any party or parties to any covered transaction may voluntarily initiate a review of the transaction by submitting a written notice of the transaction to the Chairperson of the Committee. The President or the Committee may also unilaterally initiate a review of any covered transaction or any covered transaction that has been previously reviewed if any party to the transaction submitted false or misleading material information in connection with the review, or omitted material information from information submitted to the Committee. The review must be completed before the end of the forty-five day period beginning on the date on which the investigation commenced (50 U.S.C. App. section 2170(b)(1)).

300. The Committee has the authority to take any necessary actions in connection with the transaction to protect the national security of the U.S. if the review of a covered transaction threatens to impair the national security of the U.S., is a foreign government-controlled transaction or would result in foreign control of any critical infrastructure or critical technology.[185]

II. Imports and Exports

A. *Customs*

301. Regulation of import and export commerce is a responsibility of the federal government. This task includes assessing and collecting duties, taxes and fees, and collecting accurate statistics on imported merchandise and licensing exported merchandise. Import regulation is carried out primarily by the U.S. Customs and Border Protection (CBP) under the Tariff Act of 1930 (as amended) (19 U.S.C. sections 1 et seq.), the Trade Act of 1974 (as amended) (19 U.S.C. sections 2101 et seq.), and the Customs Modernization Act (Title VI of the North American Free Trade Agreement Implementation Act [P.L. 103–182, 107 Stat. 2057]) of 1993. CBP was born in 2003 as an agency of the Department of Homeland Security, merging functions of the former U.S. Customs Service, Immigration and Naturalization Service, Border Patrol, and Animal and Plant Health Inspection Service. The Mod Act of 1993 fundamentally altered the relationship between importers and the agency that is now CBP, shifting to the importer the legal responsibility for declaring the value, classification, and rate of duty applicable to imported merchandise. The importer and CBP share a relationship of informed compliance. CBP must communicate to the importer its requirements, and the importer must exercise reasonable care in providing to CBP accurate and timely data pertaining to the importer's merchandise. The U.S. Customs Service is an agency of the U.S. Department of the Treasury. Financially, the U.S. Customs Service plays an important role in the U.S. economy. Customs provides the U.S. with its second largest source of revenue.

302. Goods imported into the U.S. must be cleared through customs. This process is referred to as "entry." Only the owner, purchaser, or licensed customs broker may "enter" the goods (19 U.S.C. section 1484). The entry process consists of filing documents necessary for U.S. Customs to determine if the goods may be released and filing the documents that enable U.S. Customs to assess applicable duties.

303. Goods imported into the U.S. are subject to duties. The particular duty rates vary depending on the goods' classification and valuation, as determined according to the Harmonized Tariff Schedule of the U.S. There are basically two types of duty rates: specific and ad valorem. A specific rate of duty is based on a specified amount per unit weight or other quantity. An ad valorem rate is a percentage of the value of the goods.

185. The decision by the Executive Branch is, however, subject to due process review by the courts. *Ralls Corp. v. Committee on Foreign Inv. in U.S.*, 758 F.3d 296 (D.D.C. 2014).

304. Classification and valuation are therefore important steps in the entry process. The Harmonized Tariff Schedule contains thousands of classifications. Since the rate of duty varies between classifications, this is an important and often contentious process. In most instances, the transaction value of the goods is used to determine the dutiable value. The transaction value is the price actually paid or payable for the good by the buyer to the seller when sold for exportation to the U.S., plus, to the extent not already included in the price, packing costs incurred by the buyer, selling commission incurred by the buyer royalty or license fees the buyer is required to pay, and proceeds accruing to the seller of any subsequent resale, disposal, or use.

305. U.S. customs law requires all goods imported into the U.S. to be conspicuously marked (legibly, indelibly, and permanently) with the English name of the country of origin. A marking duty equal to 10% of the customs value is imposed on goods that are not properly marked (19 U.S.C. section 1304). Section 42 of the Trade Mark Act of 1946 (15 U.S.C. section 1124) forbids entry into the U.S. of any good that bears a name or mark designed to induce the public to believe that it was manufactured in the U.S. or in another country other than the country in which it was actually manufactured.

B. Trade Remedies Laws

306. The Import Administration of the International Trade Administration, Department of Commerce enforces laws and agreements to protect U.S. businesses from unfair competition within the U.S. resulting from unfair pricing by foreign companies and unfair subsidies to foreign companies by their governments. These laws include the antidumping and countervailing duties laws. If a U.S. industry believes that it is being injured by unfair competition through dumping or subsidization, it may file a petition with both Import Administration and the United States International Trade Commission to request the imposition of antidumping or countervailing duties. Import Administration investigates foreign producers and governments to determine whether dumping or subsidization has occurred, and if so, in what amount. The International Trade Commission determines whether the domestic industry is suffering material injury as a result of the imports. U.S. industry petitioners must represent at least 25% of domestic production.

1. Antidumping

307. Dumping occurs when a foreign producer sells a product in the U.S. at a price that is below that producer's sales price in the country of origin or home market, or at a price that is lower than the cost of production. The difference between the price in the foreign market and that in the U.S. market is the dumping margin. The U.S. sale is dutiable if it causes or threatens to cause material injury to a competing U.S. industry. Assessed duties amount to a percentage of the value of the imports, equivalent to the dumping margin.

2. Subsidies and Countervailing Duties

308. When foreign governments provide financial assistance to benefit the production, manufacture, or exportation of goods, they subsidize industries. Subsidies can take many forms, including cash payments, credits against taxes, and loans at terms that do not reflect market conditions. When an unfair subsidy has been conferred, the subsidy is offset, or countervailed, through higher import duties based on the amount of subsidies the foreign producer receives from the foreign government.

3. Unfair Trade Practices

309. Section 337 investigations and proceedings are conducted by the U.S. International Trade Commission pursuant to 19 U.S.C. Section 1337, Unfair Practices in Import Trade. Under section 1337, unfair competition and unfair acts related to importing articles into the U.S. are unlawful. Also unlawful are unfair competition and unfair acts in the sale of imported articles by the owner, importer, or consignee when the threat or effect of the sale destroys or substantially injures a U.S. industry, prevents the establishment of a U.S. industry, or restrains or monopolizes U.S. trade and commerce. Section 1337 makes unlawful the importation, sale for importation, or sale within the U.S. after importation by the owner, importer, or consignee, of articles that infringe a valid and enforceable U.S. patent or copyright. Articles under section 1337 that are made, produced, processed, or mined under, or by means of, a process covered by the claims of a valid and enforceable U.S. patent are unlawfully imported into the U.S. Similarly unlawful are imports that infringe a valid and enforceable U.S. trademark, mask work under title 17, or exclusive rights in a design protected under title 17.

310. If the U.S. International Trade Commission determines that a violation has occurred, the Commission directs that the concerned articles be excluded from entry into the U.S., unless it finds that the articles should not be excluded. The Commission may direct that concerned articles be excluded from entry during an investigation. In addition to or in lieu of excluding articles from entry, the Commission may issue and serve on any person violating or believed to be violating section 1337 an order directing the person to cease and desist from engaging in the unfair methods or acts involved. Any person who violates an order issued by the Commission after it has become final may be required to forfeit and pay a civil penalty for each day in violation. The penalty may amount to not more than the greater of USD 100,000 or twice the domestic value of the articles entered or sold on each day violating the order.

4. Section 301 Proceedings

311. Section 301 of the U.S. Trade Act of 1974 (19 U.S.C. section 2411) authorizes the United State Trade Representative to take mandatory action as directed by the President if the rights of the U.S. under any trade agreement are denied, or if an act, policy, or practice of a foreign country violates or is inconsistent with the provisions of any U.S. trade agreement, otherwise denies benefits to the U.S. under any trade agreement, or is unjustifiable and burdens or restricts U.S. commerce. The trade representative is authorized to suspend, withdraw, or prevent the application of benefits under the concerned trade agreements. The representative may impose duties or other import restrictions on the goods of the foreign country and may impose fees or restrictions on the services of the foreign country, for such time as the trade representative deems appropriate. The representative may withdraw, limit, or suspend duty-free treatment. As well, the representative may enter into binding agreements with the foreign country that commit the foreign country to eliminate or phase out the act, policy, or practice that is the subject of the action. Agreements may also eliminate any resulting burden or restriction on U.S. commerce, or provide the U.S. with compensatory trade benefits.

C. Export Controls

312. The Bureau of Industry and Security (BIS), an agency within the U.S. Department of Commerce, is responsible for regulating the export and reexport of most commercial items under the Export Administration Regulations (EAR). The EAR does not control all goods, services, and technologies. Other U.S. government agencies regulate more specialized exports. Any item that is sent from the U.S. to a foreign destination is an export.

313. How an item is transported outside the U.S. does not matter in determining export license requirements. For example, an item can be sent by regular mail or hand-carried on an airplane, a set of schematics can be sent via facsimile to a foreign destination, software can be uploaded to or downloaded from an Internet site, or technology can be transmitted via e-mail or during a telephone conversation. Regardless of the method used for the transfer, the transaction is considered an export for export control purposes. Items are considered exports even if leaving the U.S. temporarily.

314. Though exports as defined are broad in scope, only a small percentage of total U.S. exports and reexports require export licenses. License requirements depend upon an item's technical characteristics, the destination, the end user, and the item's end use. Just as importers must determine and declare the classification, value, and duty rates for their imported merchandise, the exporter must determine whether exported merchandise requires a license, and must properly file with BIS required export documents.

315. Licensing requirements are determined based on reference to the Export Control Classification Number (ECCN) the CCL (Supplement No. 1 to EAR Part 774). The exporter can classify the item, can check with the manufacturer to determine whether the item already has an ECCN or can submit a classification request to BIS to have BIS determine the ECCN.

316. If the item falls under Commerce Department jurisdiction and is not listed on the CCL, it is designated as EAR99. EAR99 items are generally low-technology goods and do not require a license in many situations. These items are exported under the designation "NLR," signifying that "no license is required." If a license is required, a license exception may be available. If an item requires a license and no license exception is available, the exporter must apply to BIS for an export license. If the application is approved, the exporter will receive a license number and expiration date to use on export documents.

1. Sanctions

317. Violations of the EAR or any order, license or authorization issued under the EAR, are subject to the administrative sanctions described in 15 C.F.R. Section 764.3 and authorized under the amended International Emergency Economic Powers Act. Violations are also subject to any other liability, sanction, or penalty available under law. A civil monetary penalty may be imposed not to exceed the greater of USD 250,000 or an amount that is twice the amount of the transaction that is the basis of the violation. Criminal penalties may include a fine of not more than USD 1,000,000, imprisonment for not more than twenty years, or both. Other sanctions may include denial of export privileges and exclusion from practice before BIS.

2. Anti-boycott

318. BIS administers and enforces the anti-boycott provisions through its Office of Antiboycott Compliance. EAR Part 760, Restrictive Trade Practices or Boycotts, and EAR Part 762, Recordkeeping, are the anti-boycott provisions. Part 760 prohibits U.S. persons from taking or knowingly agreeing to take certain actions with intent to comply with, further, or support an unsanctioned foreign boycott. Part 760 also requires recipients of requests to take such actions to report receipt of those requests to BIS and to report whether they took the requested action. Part 762 requires retention of certain documents that contain information related to the prohibitions or reporting requirements of Part 760. EAR section 764.8 sets forth procedures for voluntary self-disclosure of anti-boycott violations. Additionally, the 26 U.S.C. Section 999 Internal Revenue Code requires a taxpayer to report whether he, a foreign corporation of which he is a U.S. shareholder, or any member of a controlled group that includes the taxpayer or the foreign corporation has participated in or cooperated with an international boycott at any time during the taxable year. The taxpayer must also report whether he received a request to participate in or cooperate with such an unsanctioned boycott and, if so, the nature of any operation connected with the boycott or request.

319. In response to an anti-boycott violation, BIS may issue a warning letter, may pursue an administrative case, or may refer a case to the DOJ for criminal prosecution. Administrative sanctions may include a monetary penalty, denial of export privileges, and an order excluding the party from practice before BIS. Violations may incur a maximum monetary penalty of USD 50,000 per violation. BIS gives voluntary self-disclosure and an effective compliance program great weight as specific mitigating factors.

III. Foreign Corrupt Practices

320. The Foreign Corrupt Practices Act of 1977 (FCPA) was enacted for the purpose of prohibiting certain classes of persons and entities from making payments to foreign government officials to assist in obtaining or retaining business and from misleading use of accounting records.[186] The antibribery provisions apply to all U.S. persons, to certain foreign issuers of securities, and to foreign firms and persons who cause, directly or through agents, an act in furtherance of such a corrupt payment to take place within the territory of the U.S. The antibribery provisions make it illegal for certain individuals and entities to offer, pay, or promise to pay any money, gift or thing of value to any foreign official for a corrupt purpose that aids the actor in obtaining or retaining business.[187] "Foreign official" includes any officer or employee of a foreign government or any department, agency, or any person acting in an official capacity for or on behalf of any such government or department.[188]

There are two important limits to the FCPA. First, it does not apply if a person charged with a violation of the FCPA's antibribery provisions may assert as an affirmative defense that the payment was lawful under the laws of the foreign country concerned. Second, it does not apply if the payment was made for the promotion of goods or services or for the performance of the specific contract for which the payments are was made.

321. The accounting provisions of the FCPA apply to companies whose securities are listed in the U.S. and require an issuer to maintain its books and records in reasonable detail and to adequately reflect the transactions and dispositions of its assets. The law also requires U.S. issuers to devise and maintain a system of internal accounting controls sufficient to provide *inter alia* reasonable assurances that transactions are executed in accordance with management's general or specific authorization and that transactions are recorded as necessary to permit preparation of financial statements in conformity with generally accepted accounting principles.

322. The extraterritorial reach of the FCPA is not readily apparent from the statutory text. The FCPA clearly applies to foreign companies whose shares are listed on any national securities exchange in the U.S.[189] even if the conduct occurs

186. 15 U.S.C. § 78dd-1, et seq.

187. *Id.*

188. 15 U.S.C. § 78dd-1(1)(A). The term "foreign official" also includes employees of state-owned companies. *Aluminum Bahrain B.S.C. V. Alcoa Inc.*, 2012 WL 2094029 (W.D. Pa. June 11, 2012); *United States v. Noriega*, No. 10-01031 (C.D. Cal. Sept. 15, 2010); *USA v. Aguilar*, 783 F. Supp. 2d 1108
(C.D. Cal. 2011).

189. *Id.* §§ 78dd-1. 78l, 78o(d).

entirely outside the U.S.[190] The FCPA also applies to a foreign national or entity that, either directly or through an agent, engages in any act in furtherance of a corrupt payment while physically in the U.S.[191] or uses any "means or instrumentality of [U.S.] interstate commerce" in furtherance of a corrupt payment is also subject to the FCPA.[192]

323. The DOJ is responsible for civil and criminal enforcement of the FCPA with respect to all domestic concerns and foreign companies and nationals. The SEC is responsible for civil enforcement with respect to issuers. Legal persons guilty of criminally infringing the FCPA may be fined up to USD 2 million per offense. Natural persons may be fined up to USD 100,000 and be imprisoned for up to five years. Actual fines for natural persons may higher under the Alternative Fines Act, amounting to up to twice the benefit that the defendant sought to obtain by making the corrupt payment. Fines imposed on natural persons may not be paid by their employers or principals. Civil actions may be brought for fines in amounts not to exceed the greater of the gross amount of the pecuniary gain to the defendant as a result of the violation, or a specified dollar limitation of up to USD 100,000 for a natural person and up to USD 500,000 for any other person. The DOJ or the SEC may also bring an action to enjoin any act or practice of a firm when it appears the firm or its representative is about to be in violation or is in violation of the act. Additionally, a person or firm found in violation of the FCPA may under guidelines issued by the Office of Management and Budget be barred from doing business with the federal government, may be ruled ineligible to receive export licenses, may under the SEC be suspended or barred from the securities business, may under the CFTC and the Overseas Private Investment Corporation be suspended or debarred from agency programs, and may not under U.S. tax laws deduct any payment unlawful under the FCPA as a business expense. Further, conduct violating the FCPA may give rise to a private cause of action for treble damages under the Racketeer Influenced and Corrupt Organization Act, or to actions under other federal or state laws.

190. *United States v. Hoskins*, 902 F.3d 69 (2d Cir. Aug. 24, 2018).
191. 15 U.S.C. § 77dd-3; *United States v. Hoskins*, 2018 WL 4038192 (2d Cir. Aug. 24, 2018).
192. 15 U.S.C. § 78dd-3(f)(5).

Chapter 3. Competition

§1. Antitrust Law

I. Sources of Antitrust Law

324. There are various sources of antitrust law in the U.S. The main statute is the Sherman Act of 1890 (15 U.S.C. section 1.). Section 1 of the Sherman Act prohibits: "Every contract, combination in the form of trust or otherwise, or conspiracy, in restraint of trade or commerce among the several states, or with foreign nations." Section 2 prohibits monopolization or the attempt to monopolize a market. Two other federal statutes that are extremely important are the Clayton Act (15 U.S.C. sections 14 et seq.) (which contains provisions on exclusive dealing, tying and mergers and acquisitions) and the Robinson-Patman Act (which prohibits various forms of discrimination) (15 U.S.C. sections 13 et seq.). As is characteristic of the U.S. federal system, these federal statutes are accompanied by numerous state statutes that address the same subject matter. The common law on restraints of trade may also be relevant—albeit to a much lesser extent.

325. The regulation of the same subject matter by both federal and state laws creates the potential for conflict. The U.S. constitutional system of government is based on the notion that the federal government has only those powers and authorities as are specifically granted to it in the Constitution or by the states. Article 1, section 8, Clause 3 of the Constitution grants the federal government the authority to regulate interstate commerce. Once the federal government has the authority to legislate, however, the Constitution provides that the Constitution and the laws of the U.S. "shall be the supreme law of the land" (Article VI, section 2). In the event of conflict, federal law preempts state law. A state law is therefore not permitted if it presents an undue burden on interstate commerce. It is the general position of the courts that the application of state antitrust law does not unduly burden interstate commerce unless the state statute is clearly discriminatory against out-of-state companies.

II. Restrictive Practices

A. Elements of the Sherman Act Section 1—Infringement

326. There are three elements to an infringement of section 1 of the Sherman Act. There must be: (1) a contract, combination or conspiracy, which (2) restrains trade or commerce and (3) has an effect on interstate commerce. Contracts, conspiracies, and combinations are not generally distinguished since the law applies to them equally.[193] In fact, they are often treated as one concept. According to the Supreme Court, the concept was meant to cover "every conceivable act" that could

193. *Northern Sec. Co. v. United States*, 193 U.S. 197 (1904).

restrain trade "without regard to the garb in which such acts were clothed."[194] Thus, it is not necessary that the contract, combination, or conspiracy be in writing.[195] The concept covers a simple understanding or meeting of the minds.[196] The standard is that "there must be direct or circumstantial evidence that reasonably tends to prove that [the parties] had a conscious commitment to a common scheme designed to achieve an unlawful objective."[197] In making this determination, the courts are instructed to look at whether the defendant had any rational motive to join the conspiracy and whether the defendant's conduct was consistent with its independent interest.[198]

327. In addition, the contract, combination, or conspiracy must be between two or more persons. Unilateral conduct is not regulated by section 1 of the Sherman Act even if it has an anticompetitive effect.[199] The coordinated activity of a parent and its wholly-owned subsidiary is considered as that of a single undertaking for purposes of the Sherman Act.[200] The basic presumption is that there is already a unity of interests between the parent and the subsidiary. This same rationale applies to agreements between two corporations belonging to the same corporate group.[201] The courts are divided on the issue of whether a parent undertaking can conspire with a subsidiary that is not wholly-owned. The test appears to be whether the parent controls the subsidiary. A shareholding of 51% or more will generally be sufficient to control a company for purposes of the intra-enterprise conspiracy doctrine.[202] The fact that the parties may be nonprofit entities does not preclude the application of the Sherman Act.[203]

328. The second element of an infringement of section 1 of the Sherman Act is that the practice must either affect trade between the states or with foreign nations. The Supreme Court has specifically stated that the authority to apply the Sherman Act is coextensive with the authority of Congress under the Commerce Clause of the United States Constitution.[204] A conspiracy can affect interstate commerce when the conduct occurred in interstate commerce or, in the event that the conduct occurred within a state, that it had an effect on interstate commerce.[205] The effect

194. *United States v. American Tobacco Co.*, 221 U.S. 106 (1911).
195. *United States v. General Motors Corp.*, 384 U.S. 127 (1966).
196. *American Tobacco Co. v. United States*, 328 U.S. 781 (1946).
197. *Monsanto Co. v. Spray-Rite Service Corp.*, 465 U.S. 752 (1984).
198. *Bell Atlantic Corp. v. Twombly*, 550 U.S. 544 (2006).
199. *American Needle, Inc. v. National Football League*, 130 S. Ct. 2201 (2010); *Fisher v. City of Berkeley*, 475 U.S. 260 (1986).
200. *American Needle, Inc. v. National Football League*, 130 S. Ct. 2201 (2010); *Copperweld Corp. v. Independence Tube Corp.*, 467 U.S. 752 (1984).
201. *Century Oil Tool, Inc. v. Production Specialties, Inc.*, 737 F.2d 1316 (1984).
202. *Novatel Communications v. Cellular Telephone Supply*, 1986-1 Trade Cases (CCH) s. 67,412 (1986).
203. *Virginia Vermiculite, Ltd. v. W.R. Grace & Co.*, 1998-2 Trade Cases (CCH) s. 72,252 (1998).
204. *Gulf Oil Corp. v. Copp Paving Co.*, 419 U.S. 186 (1974).
205. *Greenville Publishing Co. v. Daily Reflector, Inc.*, 496 F.2d 391 (1974).

must be substantial and adverse.[206] It is not necessary to show that the effect on interstate commerce was caused by the practices being contested.[207]

329. Concerted practices that have an effect on trade with foreign nations also fulfill this requirement. This is generally the case where there is an effect on imports into or exports from the U.S. The location of the parties outside the U.S. does not necessarily preclude the application of the antitrust laws if there is an effect in the U.S. or on trade with a foreign nation.[208]

330. Finally, section 1 of the Sherman Act requires that there be a restraint of trade or commerce. The concept of "trade" in this context is to be understood in its broadest sense. It covers not only the traditional notion of buying and selling but also all occupations in which people are engaged for a livelihood.[209] Moreover, the fact that the activity is not carried on for-profit does not preclude it from being considered trade within the meaning of section 1 of the Sherman Act.[210]

331. The prohibition of "every" restraint of trade contained in section 1 of the Sherman Act was initially interpreted literally by the courts.[211] This interpretation proved to be untenable since all contracts have the effect of restraining trade by limiting the commercial freedom of the parties to the contract. The Supreme Court, therefore, ruled that only those restraints that were "unreasonable" fall within the ambit of section 1 of the Sherman Act.[212] The reasonableness of a particular restraint is determined exclusively by its impact on competition.[213] In order to determine which restraints are reasonable and which are unreasonable, current U.S. antitrust jurisprudence relies on two methods of analysis: the per se rule and the rule of reason. The per se rule provides that those types of agreements whose nature and necessary effect are so plainly anticompetitive that no elaborate study of the market is needed to establish their illegality.[214] All other types of practices are subject to the rule of reason. This essentially means that their competitive effect can only be evaluated by analyzing the facts peculiar to the business, the history of the restraint, and the reasons why it was imposed.[215] According to the DOJ, the central question in applying the rule of reason is whether the agreement "likely harms competition by increasing the ability or incentive profitably to raise price above or reduce output, quality, service, or innovation below what likely would prevail in the absence

---

206. *Hospital Building Co. v. Trustees of Rex Hospital*, 425 U.S. 738 (1976).
207. *McLain v. Real Estate Board of New Orleans, Inc.*, 444 U.S. 232 (1980).
208. *Continental Ore Co. v. Union Carbide & Carbon Corp.*, 370 U.S. 690 (1962).
209. *United States v. National Association of Real Estate Boards*, 339 U.S. 485 (1950).
210. *American Medical Association v. United States*, 130 F.2d 233 (D.C. Cir. 1942).
211. *United States v. Joint Traffic Association*, 171 U.S. 505 (1898); *United States v. Trans-Missouri Freight Association*, 166 U.S. 290 (1897).
212. *Chicago Board of Trade v. United States*, 246 U.S 231 (1918); *Standard Oil v. United States*, 221 U.S. 1 (1911).
213. *Business Electronics Corp. v. Sharp Electronics Corp.*, 485 U.S. 717 (1988).
214. *Broadcast Music, Inc. v. CBS*, 441 U.S. 1 (1979); *National Society of Professional Engineers v. United States*, 435 U.S. 679 (1978).
215. *F.T.C. v. Sup. Ct. Trial Lawyers Ass'n*, 493 U.S. 411, 433 (1990); *National Soc. of Professional Engineers v. United States*, 435 U.S. 679, 692 (1978).

of the relevant agreement."[216] It is the burden of the person challenging the conduct to prove that the restraint is unreasonable.[217]

332. Although there is no *de minimis* threshold which is codified in the Sherman Act, the federal antitrust agencies have indicated that unless there are extraordinary circumstances, they will not challenge agreements when the aggregate market shares of the parties to the agreement are 20% or less on each of the affected relevant markets.[218] This does not apply, however, if the agreement is considered a per se violation of the Sherman Act.

B. Categories of Restrictive Practices

333. Horizontal Restraints: Horizontal restraints are those between firms in the same industry and at the same stage of the value chain. When dealing with such an agreement, the antitrust authorities first ask whether it is the type of restraint that is currently recognized by the courts as being a per se violation.[219] Some common forms of horizontal restraints are as follows.

334. Price Fixing: Agreements to fix prices are illegal per se under U.S. antitrust law.[220] The courts will not consider the redeeming characteristics of the practice or whether the prices fixed were reasonable.[221] Moreover, the market share of the parties is irrelevant.[222]

335. Market Allocation: Another horizontal arrangement that constitutes a per se violation of the Sherman Act is horizontal market allocation. An agreement between competitors to allocate territories or customers between them is illegal per se.[223]

336. Joint Ventures: From an antitrust law perspective, joint ventures can threaten competition in two ways. First, the formation of the joint venture may threaten the structure of competition by joining two otherwise independent firms. Second, the ongoing collaboration between the firms involved may also restrain competition between them or with third parties. Because of the potential to create

216. Antitrust Guidelines for Collaborations Among Competitors, Dep't of Justice & Fed. Trade Comm'n (2000) at s. 3.3.
217. *United States v. Schwinn*, 388 U.S. 365 (1967).
218. Antitrust Guidelines for Collaborations Among Competitors, Dep't of Justice & Fed. Trade Comm'n (2000) at s. 4.2, available at http://www.ftc.gov/os/2000/04/ftcdojguidelines.pdf; Antitr ust Guidelines for the Licensing of Intellectual Property (Apr. 6, 1995) at s. 4.3, reprinted in 4 TRADE REG. REP. (CCH) ¶13,132.
219. Antitrust Guidelines for Collaborations Among Competitors, Dep't of Justice & Fed. Trade Comm'n (2000) at s. 3.2.
220. *Arizona v. Maricopa County Medical Society*, 457 U.S. 332 (1982).
221. *United States v. McKesson & Robbins*, 351 U.S. 305 (1956).
222. *United States v. Socony-Vacuum Oil Co.*, 310 U.S. 150 (1940).
223. *Palmer v. BRG of Georgia*, 498 U.S. 46 (1990); *United States v. Topco Associates*, 405 U.S. 596 (1972); Antitrust Guidelines for Collaborations Among Competitors, Dep't of Justice & Fed. Trade Comm'n (2000) at s. 3.2.

efficiencies, however, joint ventures are analyzed under the rule of reason.[224] In the context of joint ventures, there are a number of agreements reached between the joint venture partners. If these agreements restrict competition without enhancing efficiency, they are considered "naked restraints" and prohibited per se. If, however, the agreement or concerted practice serves to promote the legitimate objectives of the joint venture, it is deemed an "ancillary restraint" and analyzed under the rule of reason.[225]

337. The rule of reason analysis applied to joint ventures is applied by shifting the burden of proof.[226] The plaintiff bears the initial burden of showing that the agreement had a substantially adverse effect on competition. Once the plaintiff meets this burden, the defendant must prove the procompetitive virtues of the conduct such as increased output, operational efficiencies or new products. If the defendant can produce such evidence, the plaintiff, in order to succeed, must prove that the conduct is not necessary to achieve the legitimate objective or there are other means available that are less restrictive of competition.

338. Exchange of Market Information between Competitors: The exchange of price information between competitors is in itself not per se illegal. As indicated above, the application of section 1 of the Sherman Act requires a contract, combination or conspiracy in restraint of trade.[227] Nonetheless, the courts tend to regard the exchange of information as a strong inference of an agreement between the parties on prices particularly when the exchange is accompanied by a pattern of parallel prices between the competitors.[228]

339. Horizontal Boycotts: The traditional approach to agreements between competitors not to deal with certain parties or boycotts was to apply the per se rule.[229] Recently, however, the Supreme Court has exhibited a willingness to take a closer look at such arrangements rather them immediately condemn them.[230]

340. Vertical Non-Price Restraints: Vertical non-price restraints are generally subject to the rule of reason.[231] Absent market power, such restraints are unlikely to be considered unreasonable. This is because the disposition of the Supreme Court that "our general view that the primary purpose of the antitrust laws is to protect interbrand competition."[232]

224. *American Needle, Inc. v. National Football League*, 130 S. Ct. 2201; *Copperweld Corp. v. Independence Tube Corp.*, 467 U.S. 752 (1984).
225. *Polk Bros., Inc. v. Forest City Enterprises, Inc.*, 776 F.2d 185 (1985).
226. *Law v. NCAA*, 134 F.3d 1010 (1998).
227. *United States v. United States Gypsum Co.*, 438 U.S. 422 (1978).
228. *North Texas Specialty Physicians v.* FTC, 528 F. 3d. 346 (5 Cir. 2008); In *re Coordinated Pretrial Proceedings & Petroleum Products Antitrust Litigation*, 906 F.2d 432 (1990).
229. *Klor's Inc. v. Broadway Hale Stores, Inc.*, 359 U.S. 207 (1959).
230. *NYNEX Corp. v. Discon, Inc.*, 525 U.S. 128 (1998).
231. *Continental T.V., Inc. v. GTE Sylvania, Inc.*, 433 U.S. 36 (1977).
232. *State Oil v. Kahn*, 522 U.S. 3 (1997); *Business Electronics Corp. v. Sharp Electronics Corp.*, 485 U.S. 717 (1988).

341. Vertical Price Restraints: Vertical price restraints refer to the practice of setting prices between actors at different levels of the supply chain. There are two types of vertical price restraints: maximum and minimum. Maximum resale price maintenance occurs when the supplier sets a maximum price above which the reseller is not allowed to resell the product or service. Minimum resale price maintenance is just the opposite; the reseller is prohibited from charging below a certain price.

342. As maximum price maintenance may have redeeming values, pursuant to federal antitrust law it is examined under the rule of reason unless the product in question has a significant market share.[233] The rationale supporting this result is that low prices benefit consumers unless they are tied to a predatory scheme.[234] There are some states, however, which continue to consider vertical maximum resale price maintenance a per se violation of state antitrust law.[235]

343. Similar to maximum resale price maintenance, minimum resale price maintenance is examined under the rule of reason.[236] The rationale employed by the Supreme Court is that "Minimum resale price maintenance can stimulate interbrand competition among manufacturers selling different brands of the same type of product by reducing intrabrand competition among retailers selling the same brand."[237]

344. Most-Favored-Customer Clauses: In certain circumstances, a supplier may want to reward its most loyal customers by agreeing to treat that customer no less favorably than it deals with its other customers. Such "most-favored-customer" agreements do not amount to unlawful price fixing.[238] However, they may be illegal if they are used to facilitate collusion between competitors who each use most-favored-customer clauses to stabilize prices.

345. Exclusive Dealing: Exclusive dealing refers to the obligation placed on a buyer of products or services to purchase those products or services exclusively from one supplier. It may also refer to the situation where the buyer agrees to purchase its requirements of a certain product or service exclusively from one supplier.

233. *State Oil v. Kahn*, 522 U.S. 3 (1997).
234. *State Oil v. Kahn*, 522 U.S. 3 (1997); *Matsushita Elec. Industrial Co. v. Zenith Radio Corp.*, 475 U.S. 574 (1986).
235. *See*, e.g., *O'Brien v. Leegin Creative Leather Products, Inc.*, 294 Kan. 318 (2012).
236. *Leegin Creative Leather Prods. Inc. v. PSKS Inc.*, 551 U.S. 877 (2007).
237. *Id.* ("A single manufacturer's use of vertical price restraints tends to eliminate intrabrand price competition; this in turn encourages retailers to invest in services or promotional efforts that aid the manufacturer's position as against rival manufacturers. Resale price maintenance may also give consumers more options to choose among low-price, low-service brands; high-price, high-service brands; and brands falling in between. Absent vertical price restraints, retail services that enhance interbrand competition might be underprovided because discounting retailers can free ride on retailers who furnish services and then capture some of the demand those services generate. Retail price maintenance can also increase interbrand competition by facilitating market entry for new firms and brands and by encouraging retailer services that would not be provided even absent free riding.").
238. *Blue Cross & Blue Shield United v. Marshfield Clinic*, 65 F.3d 1406 (1996).

Such agreements are of interest to the antitrust laws because they have the effect of foreclosing a sale opportunity to the supplier. However, they offer the buyer a secure source of supply at stable prices.

346. Exclusive dealing agreements are analyzed under a "modified" rule of reason.[239] Under the quantitative substantiability test, an anticompetitive effect exists if the exclusive arrangement forecloses a substantial portion of the market.[240] The market shares of the parties tend to be the dominant criterion under this test. The more difficult test to apply is the qualitative substantiability test. Under this test, the probable impact of the arrangement on competition in the relevant market is examined.[241] A number of relevant factors are taken into account in addition to the market shares of the parties such as the duration of the agreements, the relative strength of the parties and the nature of the product involved.

347. Exclusive Distributorships: Vertical restraints placed on a distributor as to the territory in which it may or may not sell and the customers to which it may or may not sell are analyzed under the rule or reason. The increasing reliance on global sourcing has created the incentive for suppliers to distribute directly with their suppliers. The typical situation is where a customer approaches a supplier and requests that supplier to deliver products or services to all of that customer's facilities throughout the U.S. or even the world. In its agreements with its distributors, the supplier will want to reserve the so-called national accounts for itself. The customer restraints placed on the distributor are examined under the rule of reason and tend to be permitted.[242]

348. Consignment Agreements: Consignment agreements are analyzed under the rule of reason. The Supreme Court initially held that since a consignment arrangement does not involve the transfer of title to the goods, the consignor may legally set the prices at which the product is sold.[243] Although the court has not reversed its initial decision, it has stated that the arrangement must be a bona fide consignment and not a disguised distribution network designed to fix prices.[244]

349. Dual Distribution: Dual distribution presents a challenge to the categories upon which U.S. antitrust law relies. The term "dual distribution" is used to describe the situation in which the manufacturer not only engages independent distributors to distribute its product but also acts as a distributor itself. Since the manufacturer is in competition with the independent distributors, one could argue that the distribution agreement between the independent distributor and the manufacturer is horizontal and therefore should not be analyzed under the rule of reason to the extent

---

239. *Tampa Electric Co. v. Nashville Coal Co.*, 365 U.S. 320 (1961).
240. *Standard Oil Co. v. United States*, 337 U.S. 293 (1949).
241. *Barr Labs., Inc. v. Abbott Labs.*, 978 F.2d 98 (1992).
242. *Wisconsin Music Network, Inc. v. Muzak Ltd. Partnership*, 5 F.3d 218 (1993); *White Motor Co. v. United States*, 372 U.S. 253 (1963); *Finlay & Associates, Inc. v. Borg-Warner Corp.*, 369 A.2d 541 (1977); *Snap-On Tools Corp. v. FTC*, 321 F.2d 825 (1963).
243. *United States v. General Electric*, 272 U.S. 476 (1926).
244. *Simpson v. Union Oil Company*, 377 U.S. 13 (1964).

the agreement includes price, territory or customer restrictions.[245] The courts, however, tend to characterize dual distribution systems as vertical restraints subject to the rule of reason.[246]

350. Discrimination: In general, a seller of goods or services is free to determine the prices at which it sells those goods or services. However, since the adoption of the Robinson-Patman Act in 1936, it is unlawful for any person engaged in commerce either directly or indirectly to discriminate in price between purchasers of commodities of like grade and quality if the effect of the discrimination is to substantially lessen competition (15 U.S.C. sections 13a et seq.). An infringement under the Robinson-Patman Act has eight elements:

– The sale must be in interstate commerce. This means that at least one of the sales involved crosses a state line. Price discrimination by a local seller within a state does not infringe the Robinson-Patman Act.[247] Interstate commerce is not the same as foreign commerce. Therefore, a U.S. seller may discriminate in prices between foreign buyers or even between a foreign and a domestic buyer.[248] However, discriminatory pricing to U.S. customers by a foreign seller could infringe the Robinson-Patman Act.
– There must be price discrimination. The existence of price discrimination is in most cases readily apparent because it simply means a difference in price.[249] The Supreme Court has held that the application of the Robinson-Patman Act does not depend on an anticompetitive purpose.[250] In other words, the intent of the seller is irrelevant.
– The discrimination must be between different purchasers. A seller of commodities is permitted to sell those commodities at different prices to the same purchaser. Sales between a parent and a subsidiary cannot form the basis of a successful Robinson-Patman Act claim by a third party that purchased the same goods at a higher price.[251] In addition, the actual sales must be made at different prices. Merely offering the commodities at different prices does not constitute an infringement of the Robinson-Patman Act.[252]
– The sales must also occur reasonably contemporaneous in time with each other.

This requirement ensures that the discrimination is not justified on changed circumstances such as an increase in input costs or market prices.

– The sale must be of goods or commodities. The Robinson-Patman Act does not apply to price discrimination in the context of services or intangibles.[253]

245. *Pitchford Scientific Instruments Corp. v. PEPI, Inc.*, 531 F.2d 92 (1975).
246. *Smalley & Co. v. Emerson & Cuming, Inc.*, 13 F.3d 366 (1993).
247. *McCullum v. City of Athens*, 976 F.2d 649 (1992).
248. *Zenith Radio Corp. v. Matsushita Elec. Industrial Co.*, 402 F.Supp. 244 (1975).
249. *Texaco v. Hasbrouck*, 496 U.S. 543 (1990).
250. *FTC v. Anheuser Busch, Inc.*, 363 U.S. 536 (1960).
251. *Caribe BMW v. Bayerische Motoren Werke*, 19 F.3d 745 (1994).
252. *Students Book Co. v. Washington Law Book Co.*, 232 F.2d 49 (1955).
253. *Metro Communications Co. v. Ameritech Mobile Communications*, 984 F.2d 739 (1993).

- The commodities sold must be of like grade and quality. In most cases, the commodities are identical. Problems arise, however, when slightly different goods are sold. This is a factual determination made from the perspective of the consumer. If the differences in the commodities affect the marketability and the consumer perception of such commodities, they will be considered not to be of like grade and quality. The mere fact that the commodities are sold as different brands or under different trademarks does not preclude the finding that they are of like grade and quality.[254]
- The commodities must be sold for use, consumption, or resale in the U.S. If there are only two sales involved and one of them is for export, the Robinson-Patman Act does not apply.
- The final requirement is that the effect of the price discrimination is to substantially lessen competition or tend to create a monopoly in any line of commerce or to injure, destroy, or prevent competition with any person who either grants or knowingly receives the benefit of such discrimination, or with customers or either of them. The burden of proof is on the plaintiff to prove the injury and the causal link between the injury and the price discrimination.[255] There are three types of injury that may form the basis of a valid Robinson-Patman Act claim. The term "primary line injury" refers to the injury occurring at the same level as the seller. In primary line cases, the injury is suffered by the other competitors active in the same line of distribution. "Secondary line injury" refers to the situation where the price discrimination is to competing buyers. "Third-line injury" occurs when a seller discriminates in prices to wholesalers who, as a result of the different prices, sell their products to retailers at different prices. If the retailers are competing with one another, one will be injured by the price discrimination.

351. The rule of price discrimination seems to contradict the basic tenet of competition that each seller should be able to sell its goods or services at the prices and on the terms as it chooses. In addition, it seems to ignore the fact that certain market conditions may compel a seller to charge different prices. In recognition of this contradiction, the law provides for several defenses. If the discrimination results from the good faith efforts of the seller to "meet competition," liability under the Robinson-Patman Act is precluded (15 U.S.C. section 13(b)). Similarly, it is a defense to the Robinson-Patman Act if the different prices can be explained by differences in costs associated with sales to the buyers (15 U.S.C. section 13(a)). For example, transport and delivery costs, warranty costs, and volume discounts have all been accepted as legitimate reasons for charging different prices.

352. Price discrimination is permitted under the Robinson-Patman Act if it appropriately reflects differences in costs of manufacture, sale or delivery. Price discrimination is also justified if it reflects changing conditions affecting the market or the marketability of the goods such as the imminent deterioration of perishable goods, obsolescence of seasonal goods, or sales in discontinuance of the goods.

254. *FTC v. Borden Co.*, 383 U.S. 637 (1966).
255. *Borden Co. v. FTC*, 381 F.2d 175 (1967).

353. One potential way to avoid the appearance of engaging in price discrimination would be to charge all buyers the same price but enter into brokerage relationships with certain buyers whereby they would be paid an extra brokerage commission for their efforts. From the perspective of the seller and the buyer, this would achieve the same objective as charging different prices. However, the "brokerage provision" of the Robinson-Patman Act prohibits the payment of a brokerage fee or the granting of an allowance or discount (15 U.S.C. section 13(c)).

III. Monopolization and Attempted Monopolization

354. Section 2 of the Sherman Act prohibits the practice of monopolization. This prohibition is analogous to the prohibition on abuse of a dominant position found in many other competition law regimes. The legitimate accumulation of market power is not considered illegal monopolization. Instead, it is the illegitimate use of market power that is prohibited.

355. The offense of monopolization has two elements: the possession of monopoly power in the relevant market and the willful use of that power to the detriment of competition.[256] Monopoly power is the power to control market prices or exclude competition.[257] Market share is generally the starting point in determining whether the alleged monopolist has monopoly power. A market share in excess of 70% is generally considered to be evidence of monopoly power[258] A market share below 50%, however, is generally insufficient to support an inference of monopoly power.[259] Additional factors such as barriers to market entry, relative market share, financial strength of the alleged monopolist and the other leading competitors, and the duration of the position are often taken into consideration.

356. Section 2 of the Sherman Act prohibits not only monopolization but also illegally attempting to achieve a monopoly position. The offense of attempted monopolization requires proof that the defendant has engaged in anticompetitive conduct, with a specific intent to monopolize and a dangerous probability of achieving monopoly power.[260]

357. Predatory Pricing. Predatory pricing may be considered illegal monopolization. There are two prerequisites. First, the challenged prices must be below "an appropriate measure" of the party's cost. Second, the party must have the realistic possibility of recouping its investment in the below-cost sales. In most industries, there is no economic rationale to engage in predatory pricing because there is no

---

256. *United States v. Grinnell Corp.*, 384 U.S. 563 (1966).
257. *United States v. E.I. du Pont de Nemours & Co.*, 351 U.S. 377 (1956).
258. *Hartigan v. Panhandle Pipe Line Co.*, 730 F.Supp. 826 (1990); *Heatransfer Corp. v. Volkswagenwerk AG*, 553 F.2d 964 (1977).
259. *Blue Cross & Blue Shield v. Marshfield Clinic*, 65 F.3d 1406 (1995).
260. *Spectrum Sports, Inc. v. McQuillan*, 506 U.S. 447 (1993).

opportunity to recoup the investment in the below-cost strategy. Because of the difficulty of determining what "an appropriate measure" is, courts tend to hold pricing legal if it is above that firm's average variable cost.[261]

358. Refusal to Deal. As discussed above, an agreement between competitors not to deal with another firm may be illegal. The unilateral refusal to deal may also be illegal.

359. Tying Arrangements. The practice of conditioning the sale of one product to the willingness of the customer to purchase another product is referred to as tying.[262] The practice of tying may be examined under the rule of reason or the per se rule.[263] Tying is prohibited under the rule of reason if the tying arrangement adversely affected competition.[264] Absent market power in the market of the tying product, there is unlikely going to be a sufficiently adverse effect on competition. Under the per se rule, tying is prohibited if there is (1) a tie between two separate products or services sold in separate markets; (2) the seller has sufficient economic power in the tying product market to effectuate the tying contrary to the interests of the customer; and (3) the practice has an effect on a substantial volume of commerce in the tied product market.[265] The difference between the two tests is that the per se test only applies if the firm occupies a dominant position in the market of the tying product.[266] Consequently, tying cases tend to center on the issue of whether the seller has sufficient economic power to restrain trade in the market for the tied product. This is generally a question of fact that must be decided in each case. However, the market share of the seller in the market of the tying product is an important consideration. Absent a significant market share in this market, it is unlikely that the court will find the existence of an illegal tying arrangement.

360. Patent Prosecution. In general, the enforcement by a patent holder of his or her rights to preclude others from making or selling a particular product does not infringe the antitrust laws even if the patent holder holds market power.[267] If, however, the patent was obtained through fraud,[268] or the suit is a mere sham to

261. *MCI Communications Corp. v. AT&T*, 708 F.2d 1081 (1982); *Morgan v. Ponder*, 892 F.2d 1355 (1989).

262. *Northern Pac. Ry. Co. v. United States*, 356 U.S. 1, 5–6 (1958); *Cascade Health Solutions v. PeaceHealth*, 515 F.3d 883, 912 (9th Cir.2008); *Datel Holdings Ltd. v. Microsoft Corp.*, 712 F.Supp.2d 974, 995 (N.D.Cal.2010).

263. *Sidibe v. Sutter Health*, 4 F.Supp.3d 1160 (2013); *Tucker v. Apple Computer, Inc.*, 493 F.Supp.2d 1090 (N.D. Ca. 2006).

264. *Jefferson Parish Hosp. Dist. v. Hyde*, 466 U.S. 2, 31 (1984); *Sidibe v. Sutter Health*, 4 F.Supp.3d 1160 (N.D. Ca. 2013); *Brantley v. NBC Universal, Inc.*, 675 F.3d 1192, 1197 (9th Cir.2012).

265. *Sidibe v. Sutter Health*, 4 F.Supp.3d 1160, 1177 (N.D. Ca. 2013); *Tucker v. Apple Computer, Inc.*, 493 F.Supp.2d 1090, 1096 (N.D. Ca. 2006).

266. The mere fact that the firm holds a patent over the tying product is not sufficient to fulfill this requirement. *Illinois Tool Works Inc. v. Independent Ink, Inc.*, 547 U.S. 28 (2006).

267. *Intergraph Corp. v. Intel Corp.*, 195 F.3d 1346, 1362 (Fed. Cir. 1999); *Handguards, Inc. v. Ethicon, Inc.* 601 F.2d 986, 993 (9th Cir. 1979).

268. *Walker Process Equipment, Inc. v. Food Machinery & Chemical Corp.*, 382 U.S. 172, 177 (1965).

cover an attempt to prevent a potential competitor from entering the market, the litigation may be deemed anticompetitive.[269]

IV. Mergers and Acquisitions

361. Section 7 of the Clayton Act prohibits the acquisition by any person of all or part of the stock or assets of another person where in any line of commerce in any section of the country the effect of such acquisition may be substantial to lessen competition or tend to create a monopoly (15 U.S.C. section 18). In addition, the persons must be engaged in interstate or foreign commerce or in any activity affecting interstate or foreign commerce.

362. Whenever the FTC has reason to believe that a corporation is violating, or is about to violate, section 7 of the Clayton Act, the FTC may seek a preliminary injunction to prevent a merger pending the administrative adjudication of the merger's legality (15 U.S.C. section 5(b)). First, the government must show that the merger would produce a firm controlling an undue percentage share of the relevant market, and would result in a significant increase in the concentration of firms in that market.[270] The Herfindahl-Hirschman index (HHI) is often used to assess the extent of concentration in an industry. The index is merely the sum of the squares of the market shares of the fifty latest participants in a particular market. That equation will result in an integer that is used by the antitrust authorities as a benchmark. Generally, a concentration index of 1,500 or less will not be challenged by the government. If the index is above 1,500 the government will probably the merger if it increases the index more than 100 points.[271] In markets where the merger would result in an HHI of above 2,500, there is a presumption of dominance if the delta is above 200.

363. A showing that the merger would result in a significant increase in the concentration of firms in that market establishes a "presumption" that the merger will substantially lessen competition.[272] To rebut the presumption, the defendants must produce evidence that shows that the market share statistics give an inaccurate account of the merger's probable effects on competition in the relevant market.[273] The majority of courts have considered efficiencies as a means to rebut the government's prima facie case that a merger will lead to restricted output or increased prices. If the defendant successfully rebuts the presumption of illegality, the burden

269. *Otter Tail Power Co. v. United States*, 410 U.S. 366, 379-80 (1973); *California Motor Transport Co. v. Trucking Unlimited*, 404 U.S. 508, 510 (1972); *Nobelpharma AB v. Implant Innovations, Inc.*, 141 F.3d 1059, 1068 (Fed. Cir. 1998).
270. *United States v. Baker Hughes Inc.*, 908 F.2d 981, 982–83 (1990).
271. U.S. Dept. of Justice and FTC, Horizontal Merger Guidelines (Aug. 19, 2010). It should be noted, however, that not all courts have accepted this approach as an adequate indication of concentration in an industry for antitrust purposes. *United States v. Black & Decker Manufacturing Co.*, 430 F.Supp. 729 (1976).
272. *United States v. Baker Hughes*, 908 F.2d 981, 982 (1990).
273. *United States v. Citizens & S. Nat'l Bank*, 422 U.S. 86, 120 (1975).

of producing additional evidence of anticompetitive effect shifts to the government, and merges with the ultimate burden of persuasion which remains with the government at all times.[274]

V. Antitrust Immunities

364. Judicially Created Antitrust Immunities: State Action Doctrine. The Sherman Act only applies to persons. As the Supreme Court has stated, this limitation on the scope of the act precludes its application to the federal government.[275] The general rule is that the antitrust laws do not apply to action by a state acting in its sovereign capacity or to private conduct that is compelled by the state.[276] The requirements for the application of the doctrine depend on the level of state action. If the action is by the state legislature or the court in its legislative or judicial capacity, the application of the doctrine to preclude the application of the antitrust laws is automatic.[277] If the action is by a state agency or local government body, the doctrine only applies if the action is taken pursuant to a state policy that is "clearly articulated and affirmatively expressed."[278] In the event that the challenged conduct is by a private party in accordance with state law or policy, not only must the action be pursuant to a clearly articulated and affirmatively expressed public policy but it must also be subject to active state supervision.[279] The mere potential for state supervision is insufficient to invoke the doctrine.[280]

365. Although the state may infringe the antitrust laws under certain circumstances, the federal government has reduced the exposure of local governments and officials. In 1984, Congress adopted the Local Government Antitrust Immunity Act that prevents collection of damages under the federal antitrust laws from any local government including its officials and employees as long as they are acting in their official capacity (15 U.S.C. sections 34 et seq.).

366. Judicially Created Antitrust Immunities: Noerr-Pennington Doctrine. In *Eastern Railroad Conference v. Noerr Motor Freight*[281] railroad companies conspired to lobby Congress to pass laws that harmed their competitors, that is, trucking companies. Despite the fact that this conduct had the effect of injuring competition, the Supreme Court held that it did not fall under the Sherman Act. The doctrine that acts directed at the political branches of government are protected even if they injure competition was confirmed in *United Mine Workers of American v. Pennington,* which involved efforts by large mining companies to sets minimum

274. *United States v. Baker Hughes Inc.*, 908 F.2d 981, 983 (1990).
275. *United States v. Cooper*, 312 U.S. 600 (1941).
276. *Parker v. Brown*, 317 341 (1943); *Hoover v. Ronwin*, 466 U.S. 558 (1984); *Massachusetts School of Law at Andover v. American Bar Association*, 107 F.3d 1026 (1997).
277. *Columbia Steel Casting Co. v. Portland General Electric Co.*, 60 F.3d 1390 (1995).
278. *Town of Hallie v. City of Eau Claire*, 471 U.S. 34 (1985).
279. *Southern Motor Carriers Rate Conference, Inc. v. US*, 471 U.S. 48 (1985).
280. *FTC v. Ticor Title Insurance Co.*, 504 U.S. 621 (1992).
281. 365 U.S. 127 (1961).

wages in the industry so high that it was difficult for smaller competitors to competitively hire employees.[282] This doctrine was later extended to cover administrative petitions and lawsuits.[283]

367. The protection accorded by the Noerr-Pennington Doctrine is subject to abuse. A company can impose significant costs on its smaller rivals by instituting proceedings that have no objective basis. For example, the lobbying activities of U.S. companies resulting in antidumping proceedings imposing costs on foreign competitors are protected by the doctrine.[284] The courts have therefore refused to extend the Noerr-Pennington Doctrine to "sham" petitions or lawsuits.[285] In order to qualify as a sham, the lawsuit must be "objectively baseless." A lawsuit is objectively baseless if no reasonable litigant could realistically expect success on the merits. In addition, the baseless lawsuit must be intended to conceal an attempt to interfere directly with the business relationship between competitors through the use of governmental process.

368. Statutory Exemptions. In addition to the judicially created exemptions, Congress has determined that certain sectors of the economy should be exempt from the antitrust laws. For example, cooperative associations of persons engaged in the production of agricultural products,[286] state-regulated insurance companies,[287] agreements in the field of sports to jointly sell broadcasting rights.[288] In addition, organized labor enjoys exemption for many of its activities.[289]

VI. Enforcement

369. The U.S. relies on a combination of public and private enforcement to secure compliance with its antitrust laws. At the federal level, the primary public enforcement agency is the DOJ. Within the DOJ, the Antitrust Division is charged specifically with enforcement of the antitrust laws. The DOJ has exclusive authority to enforce the Sherman Act. It shares its authority to enforce the Clayton Act with the FTC.

370. The FTC is an independent federal agency composed of five Commissioners appointed by the President for seven-year terms. It is subdivided into three bureaus: the Bureau of Competition, the Bureau of Consumer Protection, and the Bureau of Economics. Although it shares authority to enforce the Clayton Act with the DOJ, it has exclusive authority to enforce the FTC Act.

282. 381 U.S. 657 (1965).
283. *California Motor Transport Co. v. Trucking Unlimited*, 404 U.S. 508 (1972).
284. *Cheminor Drugs, Ltd. v. Ethyl Corp.*, 168 F.3d 119 (1999).
285. *Professional Real Estate Investors v. Columbia Pictures*, 508 U.S. 49 (1993).
286. Capper-Volstead Act, 7 U.S.C. s. 291.
287. McCarran-Ferguson Act, 15 U.S.C. ss. 1011 et seq.
288. Sports Broadcasting Act, 15 U.S.C. s. 1291.
289. 15 U.S.C. s. 17; 29 U.S.C. s. 52.

371. In addition, the attorney generals in the respective states may enforce the antitrust laws. Since a state qualifies as a "person" under the Clayton Act, it may sue for treble damages and seek injunctive relief.[290] The Hart-Scott-Rodino Antitrust Improvements Act ('HSR Act') of 1976 gave the states *parens patriae* authority to sue on behalf of injured citizens within its territory (15 U.S.C. section 15c). In practice, the enforcement activities of the states in the field of antitrust are coordinated in the framework of the Multistate Antitrust Task Force of the National Association of Attorneys General.

372. Most of the enforcement mechanisms relied upon by the antitrust agencies are remedial in nature. The primary enforcement mechanism available to the enforcement agencies is a civil action against the perpetrators. The Clayton Act allows the DOJ and the FTC to institute civil proceedings for infringements of the antitrust laws. The DOJ may initiate an action for treble damages (15 U.S.C. section 15a) or injunctive relief (15 U.S.C. section 25). In addition, the DOJ may institute criminal proceedings for certain infringements. In the event that a corporation violates the penal provisions of the antitrust laws, the directors, officers, or agents directly involved in such violation are held personally liable if that person knowingly participated in the violation.[291]

373. Because of the difficulties of identifying and dismantling concentrations, however, the antitrust agencies were given preventative authorities to review certain types of transactions creating a change in the structure of the market. The "HSR Act" requires that parties to certain mergers and acquisitions notify such transactions to the FTC and the U.S. DOJ prior to consummating the transaction.

374. In order to determine which transactions have to be notified, the HSR Act employs a "size-of-person" test and a "size-of-transaction" test. With one exception, a transaction must be notified only if it meets both of these tests. Although these thresholds are adjusted annually for inflation (or deflation), the current size-of-the-parties test is met if one person has worldwide sales or worldwide assets of at least USD 161.5 million and the other person has worldwide sales or worldwide assets of at least USD 16.2 million. The size-of-transaction-test is met if the acquiring person is acquiring assets with a value of USD 80.8 million or more or, if as a result of the transaction, the acquiring person would hold an aggregate total amount of the voting securities and assets of the acquired person in excess of USD 80.8 million. Certain major transactions may have to be notified to the FTC and DOJ under the HSR Act even if the size-of-person test and the size-of-transaction test are not met. A notification is automatically required for all transactions with a value in excess of USD 323 million.

375. Once the transaction has been properly notified, and the filing fee paid, a thirty-day waiting period begins. During this time, the parties cannot close the transaction unless the antitrust authorities have granted early termination of the waiting

290. *Georgia v. Pennsylvania R.R.*, 324 U.S. 439 (1945).
291. *United States v. Wise*, 370 U.S. 405 (1962).

period. The waiting period may be extended in the event that the antitrust authorities determine that they would like to take a closer look at the proposed transaction.

376. As discussed above, the U.S. antitrust laws rely on a combination of public and private enforcement to secure compliance. One of the unique aspects of U.S. antitrust law is the degree to which it relies on private individuals for its enforcement. An infringement of the U.S. antitrust laws can give rise to several remedies available to the private plaintiff. The most impressive remedy available is treble damages under section 4 of the Clayton Act (15 U.S.C. section 15). In addition, the private plaintiff may seek injunctive relief under section 16 of the Clayton Act (15 U.S.C. section 26).

377. The institution of a case by the government does not preclude a private claim.[292] One basic requirement for a plaintiff to bring a claim based on an alleged violation of the antitrust laws is that the plaintiff has standing to bring the claim. Standing means that the plaintiff has suffered "antitrust injury." In other words, the plaintiff must have suffered (or immediately threatened by) the type of injury that the legal norm on which the claim is based was intended to prevent. For example, a competitor of two firms engaged in horizontal price fixing cannot bring a claim against the conspiring firms based on the antitrust laws because the customers, and not the competitor, suffered the injury.[293]

VII. Extraterritorial Jurisdiction

378. U.S. antitrust laws apply even to conduct that occurs outside of the U.S. provided that there is an effect in the U.S.[294] If the foreign conduct does not involve import commerce, the Sherman Act only applies to the foreign conduct if such conduct: (1) has a direct, substantial, and reasonably foreseeable effect on: (i) trade or commerce that is not trade or commerce with foreign nations, or on import trade or import commerce with foreign nations; or (ii) on export trade or export commerce with foreign nations, of a person engaged in such trade or commerce in the U.S.; and (2) such effect gives rise to a Sherman Act claim.[295] Otherwise the test for the extraterritorial reach of the Sherman Act to foreign conduct is whether the conduct was intended to and did produce some substantial effect in the U.S.[296] A U.S. court may, however, in its discretion, decline to apply the antitrust laws to foreign conduct or foreign persons if such application would violate principles of comity or international law.[297]

292. *United States v. US Gypsum Co.*, 51 F.Supp. 613 (1943).
293. *Matsushita Elec. Indus. Co. v. Zenith Radio Corp.*, 475 U.S. 574 (1986).
294. *United States v. Aluminum Co. of America*, 148 F.2d 416 (1945).
295. Foreign Trade Antitrust Improvements Act of 1982, 15 U.S.C.S. s. 6a (2002); *F. HoffmannLaRoche v. Empagran S.A.*, 542 U.S. 155 (2004).
296. *Hartford Fire Insurance Co. v. California*, 509 U.S. 764 (1993).
297. *Timberlane Lumber Co. v. Bank of America, N.T. & S.A.*, 549 F.2d 597 (1977).

§2. UNFAIR COMPETITION AND TRADE PRACTICES

I. Unfair and Deceptive Trade Practices under the FTC Act

A. *Federal Trade Commission Act*

379. The main federal statute dealing with unfair competition and unfair trade practices is the FTC Act (15 U.S.C. section 45(a)). This law is supplemented by common law and numerous state statutes that address the same types of practices.

380. The FTC Act prohibits unfair methods of competition and unfair or deceptive acts or practices in or affecting interstate or foreign commerce (15 U.S.C. section 45(a)(1)). The law entrusts the FTC with its enforcement. A major purpose of this act was to enable the FTC to restrain practices as unfair that, although not yet constituting violations of the Sherman Act, would likely to do so if left unrestrained.[298]

381. The affecting commerce requirement means that the law does not apply to commerce with foreign nations unless one of three conditions is present: (1) there is an effect on import commerce; (2) there is a direct, substantial, and reasonably foreseeable effect on commerce that is not commerce with foreign nations; or (3) there is a direct, substantial, and reasonably foreseeable effect on export commerce with foreign nations of a person engaged in such commerce in the U.S. (15 U.S.C. section 45(a)(3)).

382. The expression "unfair methods of competition" used in the act has a broader meaning than common law unfair competition.[299] It is not confined to fraud or other acts illegal at common law (15 U.S.C. section 45(a)(1)).

383. The FTC Act (15 U.S.C. section 45(a)(1)) extends to violations of the Sherman and Clayton Acts.[300] Proceedings are frequently brought under the act against conduct violating the Sherman Act. Although all Sherman Act violations constitute violations of the FTC Act, the converse is not necessarily true.[301] Many unfair methods of competition do not rise to the level of Sherman Act violations.

II. Interference with Contractual Relations

384. Under the common law, a person or business that induces another person or business to breach a contract to which the latter is a party may incur liability to the other party or parties to the contract.[302] The liability is based not on contract but

298. *Federal Trade Commission v. Cement Institute*, 334 U.S. 839 (1948).
299. *ALA Schechter Poultry Corp. v. United States*, 295 U.S. 495 (1935).
300. *Times-Picayune Pub. Co. v. United States*, 345 U.S. 594 (1953).
301. *FTC v. Cement Institute*, 333 US 683 (1948).
302. *American Surety Co. v. Schottenbauer*, 257 F.2d 6 (1958).

rather on tort.[303] The particular contract must be valid and in force at the time of the inducement to breach and the breach itself. Mere conduct arising in the breach is not sufficient. The actor must intend to induce the breach.

385. The intentional interference in precontractual relations can also lead to liability under the common law if the interference leads to the loss of the benefits of the contractual relationship that would have otherwise occurred.[304] The interference generally occurs in the form of inducing or otherwise causing the third person not to enter into the contract.

386. Interference in the business relationships of others can also result in tort liability. The elements of this tort are similar to interference in the contractual relations. The difference is that instead of a contract, it is only necessary to prove that a business relationship existed.[305] The tort grew out of attempts to counteract the threat of violence to deter customers from doing business with another individual.

387. In determining whether an actor's conduct in intentionally interfering with a contract or a prospective contractual relation of another is improper, consideration is given to the following factors: the nature of the actor's conduct, the actor's motive, the interest of the other with which the actor's conduct interferes, the interest sought to be advanced by the actor, the social interests in protecting the freedom of action of the actor and the contractual interests of the other, the proximity or remoteness of the actor's conduct to the interference and the relations between the parties.[306]

388. A person who is found liable to another person for interference with a contract or prospective contractual relation is liable for damages for the pecuniary loss of the benefits of the contract or the prospective relation and consequential losses for which the interference is a legal cause. That person is also liable for emotional distress or actual harm to reputation if they are reasonably to be expected to result from the interference.[307]

III. Price Misrepresentations

389. It is an unfair or deceptive practice in violation of the FTC Act to make any false representation as to the price of goods if the representation has a capacity or tendency to deceive or mislead the purchaser in making his or her decision whether

---

303. *Lumley v. Gye*, 118 Eng. Rep. 749 (1853).
304. Restatement Torts (Second) s. 766B.
305. *Okusami v. Psychiatric Inst. of Washington*, 959 F.2d 1062 (1992); *Longo v. Reilly*, 114 A.2d 302 (1955).
306. Restatement Torts (Second) s. 767.
307. *Id.*, s. 774.

to buy.[308] That the misrepresentation is obviously false to those who are trained and experienced does not change its illegal character if it has a tendency to deceive others less experienced and trained.[309]

390. The prohibition on unfair trade extends also to deceptive pricing practices. Under the FTC's Guides Against Deceptive Pricing, it is an unfair trade practice to represent that the price of a product or service has been reduced from what is, in fact, a fictitious price or to represent that a price is a reduced or a special price when it is, in fact, the regular selling price of the product. It is also considered deceptive to make false or misleading price comparisons, or otherwise falsely or deceptively to represent the past or current price of a product or service (16 C.F.R. sections 233.1 et seq.).

IV. Product Misrepresentations

391. Product misrepresentations may also be the basis of a cause of action. The following types of product misrepresentation have been held to be actionable:

- misrepresenting the nature of products;[310]
- misrepresenting product performance;[311]
- misrepresenting the creator of the product;[312]
- misrepresenting the method of manufacture;[313]
- misrepresenting composition or contents;[314]
- misrepresenting geographical origin.[315]

V. Injurious Falsehood

392. In the U.S., a person who publishes a false statement harmful to the interests of another person or legal entity may be subject to liability for the resulting pecuniary loss if the publication of the statement was intended to result in harm to interests of the other having a pecuniary value (or either recognizes or should recognize that it is likely to do so), and the person knows that the statement is false or acts in reckless disregard of its truth or falsity.[316] Publication of an injurious falsehood in this context means the communication of the statement to someone other

308. *Regina Corp. v. Federal Trade Com.* 322 F.2d 765 (1963); *De Gorter v. Federal Trade Com.* 244 F.2d 270 (1957).
309. *FTC v. Standard Education Soc.*, 302 U.S. 112 (1937).
310. *FTC v. Think Achievement Corp.*, 144 F.Supp. 2d 993 (2000).
311. *Chrysler v. FTC*, 561 F.2d 357 (1977).
312. *Niresk Industries v. FTC*, 278 F. 2d 337 (1960).
313. *FTC v. Maisel Trading Post*, 77 F. 2d 246 (1935).
314. *FTC v. Algoma Lumber Co.*, 291 U.S. 67 (1934).
315. *American Tack Co. v. FTC*, 211 F. 2d 239 (1954).
316. Restatement Torts (Second) s. 623A.

than the person whose interest is affected.[317] In other words, if a statement qualifying as a falsehood is communicated only to the person to whom it relates, there is no publication.

393. In an action for injurious falsehood the plaintiff has the burden of proving the injurious character of the falsehood, publication of the falsehood, the falsity of the statement, and the pecuniary loss resulting from the publication.[318]

VI. Deceptive Marketing

394. One who, in connection with the marketing of goods or services, makes a representation relating to the actor's own goods, services, or commercial activities that is likely to deceive or mislead prospective purchasers to the likely commercial detriment of another may be subject to liability to the other.[319] The rationale for this rule is that unless prospective purchasers can accurately compare the products offered by competing sellers, the free enterprise system cannot operate efficiently. The use of deceptive representations in the marketing of goods and services impairs the ability of purchasers to choose intelligently among competing products. As confidence in the truth of advertising diminishes, prospective purchasers may be forced to expend additional resources in examining and sampling competing products.

395. In addition to the common law of unfair competition discussed above, federal law (section 43[a] of the Lanham Act (15 U.S.C. section 1125[a]) prohibits any person who, on or in connection with any goods or services, or any container for goods, uses in commerce any word, term, name, symbol or device, or any combination thereof, or any false designation of origin, false or misleading description of fact or false or misleading representation of fact, which: (1) is likely to cause confusion, or to cause mistake, or to deceive as to the affiliation, connection or association of such person with another person, or as to the origin, sponsorship, or approval of his or her goods, services or commercial activities by another person; or (2) in commercial advertising or promotion, misrepresents the nature, characteristics, qualities or geographic origin of his or her or another person's goods, services or commercial activities, shall be liable in a civil action by any person who believes that he or she is or likely to be damaged by such act.[320]

396. There are essentially five elements to a false or misleading advertising claim under the Lanham Act:

– the defendant must have made a false statement or representation of a material fact about a product in the context of commercial advertising or promotion;

317. *General Electric v. Sargent & Lundy*, 916 F. 2d 1119 (1992).
318. Restatement Torts (Second) s. 651; *Auvil v. CBS*, 67 F.3d 816 (1995).
319. Restatement Unfair Competition (Third) s. 2.
320. There is no requirement for a claim for deceptive marketing under s. 43(a) of the Lanham Act that the plaintiff has actually used the trademark in the U.S. *Belmora LLC v. Bayer Consumer Care AG*, 819 F.3d 697 (2016).

- the statement creates either actual deception or at least a deceptive impression among a substantial section of the audience to whom the advertisement is directed;
- the deception must be material in that it is likely to influence consumers' purchasing decisions;
- the advertised goods traveled in interstate commerce; and
- there is a likelihood of injury, stemming either from a decline in sales or a loss in goodwill.

397. A statement of opinion, even if included in a commercial advertisement, is not actionable under the Lanham Act if it could not reasonably be seen as stating or implying provable facts.[321] The basic remedies for a breach of the Lanham Act are damages and an injunction prohibiting the dissemination of advertisements making the wrongful claim. Any "person" who is damaged is entitled to sue. In order to claim damages, however, the plaintiff must prove the defendant's intent to deceive or that it suffered actual injury caused by the defendant's false advertising.

VII. Passing Off

398. Another form of deceptive marketing is passing off. One is subject to liability to another if, in connection with the marketing of goods or services, the actor makes a representation likely to deceive or mislead prospective purchasers by causing the mistaken belief that the actor's business is the business of the other, or that the actor is the agent, affiliate, or associate of the other, or that the goods or services that the actor markets are produced, sponsored, or approved by the other.[322]

VIII. Infringement of Marks and Trade Names

399. Liability for trademark or trade name infringement arises if the infringing individual uses a designation that causes a likelihood of confusion that the individual's business is the business of the other or is associated or otherwise connected with the other.[323] A party proves trademark infringement by showing: (1) that it owns a trademark, (2) that the infringer used the mark in commerce without authorization, and (3) that the use of the alleged infringing trademark "is likely to cause confusion among consumers regarding the origin of the goods offered by the parties."[324] Infringement may also arise if the infringing individual creates the impression that the goods or services marketed by him or her are produced, sponsored,

---

321. *Boule v. Hutton*, 2003–2 CCH Trade Cases ¶74,095 (2d Cir. 2003).
322. Restatement Unfair Competition (Third) s. 4.
323. 15 U.S.C. s. 1114(a)(a).
324. *Coach, Inc. v. Frederick Goodfellow*, 717 F.3d 498 (6th Cir. 2013); *Leelanau Wine Cellars, Ltd. v. Black & Red, Inc.*, 502 F.3d 504, 515 (6th Cir. 2007 (quoting *Daddy's Junky Music Stores, Inc. v. Big. Daddy's Family Music Ctr.*, 109 F.3d 275, 280 (6th Cir. 1997)).

certified, or approved by the other or that the goods or services marketed by the individual are produced, sponsored, certified, or approved by the trademark holder.[325] An online marketplace may be liable for contributory trademark infringement if it knew or had reason to know identified vendors were engaging in infringing activity.[326]

400. Proof of Likelihood of Confusion: Market Factors. Whether an individual's use of a designation causes a likelihood of confusion with the use of a trademark or trade name by another is determined by a consideration of all the circumstances involved in the marketing of the respective goods or services or in the operation of the respective businesses. In making that determination the following market factors, among others, may be important.[327]

- the degree of similarity between the respective designations;
- the degree of similarity in the marketing methods and channels of distribution used for the respective goods or services;
- the characteristics of the prospective purchasers of the goods or services and the degree of care they are likely to exercise in making purchasing decisions;
- the degree of distinctiveness of the other's designation;
- when the goods, services, or business of the actor differ in kind from those of the other, the likelihood that the actor's prospective purchasers would expect a person in the position of the other to expand its marketing or sponsorship into the product, service, or business market of the actor;
- when the actor and the other sell their goods or services or carry on their businesses in different geographic markets, the extent to which the other's designation is identified with the other in the geographic market of the actor.

IX. Trademark Counterfeiting

401. Trademark counterfeiting refers to an attempt to "pass off" replica products as genuine goods.[328] A claim for direct trademark counterfeiting requires the plaintiff to show: (1) ownership of a valid trademark, and (2) a defendant's use of that trademark in connection with the sale of goods, without authorization from the trademark owner, that is likely to cause confusion, deception, or mistake.[329] An offer to sell counterfeit goods without more will suffice to establish liability.[330] In

325. Restatement Unfair Competition (Third) s. 20.
326. *Coach, Inc. v. Frederick Goodfellow*, 717 F.3d 498 (6th Cir. 2013); *Rosetta Stone*, 676 F.3d at 163-65; *Tiffany (NJ), Inc. v. eBay, Inc.*, 600 F.3d 93, 105-10 (2d Cir. 2010).
327. Restatement Unfair Competition (Third) s. 21.
328. *Chloe SAS v. Sawabeh Information Services Co.*, (C.D. Ca. Oct. 8, 2013).
329. 15 U.S.C. s. 1114(1); *Gucci Am. Inc. v. Pieta*, No. CV 04-9626, 2006 WL 4725706, at *3 (C.D. Cal. Jan 23, 2006).
330. *Chloe SAS v. Sawabeh Information Services Co.*, (C.D. Ca. Oct. 8, 2013); *Levi Strauss & Co. v. Shilon*, 121 F.3d 1309, 1312 (9th Cir. 1997).

assessing a counterfeit trademark claim, it is unnecessary to perform the likelihood of confusion examination because counterfeit marks are inherently confusing.[331]

A claim for contributory counterfeiting requires the plaintiff to show direct counterfeiting and that they continued to supply services to the counterfeiter who they knew or had reason to know was engaging in trademark infringement.[332] If a website host is aware of products being sold on its platform which are counterfeit, for example, the website host may be held liable for contributory counterfeiting.

X. Trademark Dilution

402. Liability for trademark infringement generally requires proof that the actor's use causes a likelihood of confusion. A number of states, however, have created a statutory cause of action for trademark "dilution"—a theory of liability that does not require proof of a likelihood of confusion. These "antidilution" statutes protect the commercial value or "selling power" of a mark by prohibiting uses that dilute the distinctiveness of the mark or tarnish the associations evoked by the mark.

XI. Appropriation of Trade Secrets

403. In general, a trade secret is any information that can be used in the operation of a business or other enterprise and that is sufficiently valuable and secret to afford an actual or potential economic advantage over others.[333] Under the UTSA, which has been adopted by the majority of states a trade secret is information, including a formula, pattern, compilation, program, device, method, technique, or process, that derives independent economic value, actual or potential, from not being generally known to, and not being readily ascertainable by proper means by, other persons who can obtain economic value from its disclosure or use, and is the subject of efforts that are reasonable under the circumstances to maintain its secrecy.[334] Information that is publicly known is not a trade secret even though it may belong to a particular company.[335]

404. A person to whom a trade secret has been disclosed owes a duty of confidence to the owner of the trade secret if the person made an express promise of confidentiality prior to the disclosure of the trade secret. The duty of confidence also exists if the trade secret was disclosed to the person under circumstances in which the relationship between the parties to the disclosure or the other facts surrounding the disclosure indicate that the person knew or had reason to know that the disclosure was intended to be in confidence.[336]

331. *Phillip Morris USA Inc. v. Shalabi*, 352 F.Supp. 2d 1067, 1073 (C.D. Cal. 2004); *Chloe SAS v. Sawabeh Information Services Co.*, (C.D. Ca. Oct. 8, 2013).
332. *Louis Vuitton Malletier, S.A. v. Akanoc Solutions, Inc.*, 658 F.3d 936 (9th Cir. 2011).
333. Restatement (Third) of Unfair Competition § 39 (1995).
334. Uniform Trade Secrets Act § 1(4).
335. *Big Vision Private Ltd. v. E.I. DuPont De Nemours & Co.*, 1 F.Supp. 3d 224 (S.D. N.Y. 2014).
336. Restatement Unfair Competition (Third) s. 41.

405. The appropriation of another person's trade secrets may result in liability if it is acquired by improper means. The UTSA identifies two types of misappropriation. First, misappropriate occurs when a person acquires a trade secret of another by a person who knows or has reason to know that the trade secret was acquired by improper means. Second, misappropriate occurs upon disclosure or use of a trade secret of another without express or implied consent by a person who either used improper means to acquire knowledge of the trade secret or, at the time of disclosure or use, knew or had reason to know that his knowledge of the trade secret was derived from or through a person who had utilized improper means to acquire it or, before a material change of his or her position, knew or had reason to know that it was a trade secret and that knowledge of it had been acquired by accident or mistake.[337]

In Texas, for example, to succeed on a claim for misappropriation of trade secrets, a plaintiff must demonstrate: (1) the existence and ownership of a trade secret, (2) the breach of a confidential relationship or improper discovery of a trade secret, (3) use or disclosure of a trade secret, and (4) damages to the owner.[338] As the Supreme Court of Texas explained in *In re Bass*, these factors include: (1) the extent to which the information is known outside the business of the entity claiming the trade secret, (2) the extent to which it was known by employees and others involved in the business, (3) the extent of the measures taken by the entity to guard the secrecy of the information, (4) the value of the information to the entity and its competitors, (5) the amount of effort or money expended by the entity in developing the information, and (6) the ease or difficulty with which the information could be properly acquired or duplicated by others.[339]

XII. Cybersquatting

406. The Anticybersquatting Consumer Protection Act (15 U.S.C. section 1125(d)) amends the Lanham Act to give trademark owners a direct cause of action against cybersquatting and applies retroactively to domain names registered before November 29, 1999. Liability is established if a person, in bad faith, registers, traffics in, or uses a domain name that is: (1) identical or confusingly similar to an already distinctive trademark; or (2) identical or confusingly similar to or dilutive of an already famous trademark. The bad faith requirement ensures that liability will not be imposed on domain name registrants who act in good faith.[340] If, for example, the domain name is used in the selling of goods or services or consists of the legal name of that person, the inference is that the person acted in good faith.

407. In addition, the Anticybersquatting Consumer Protection Act specifically provides for in rem actions, that is, actions against the domain itself, rather than the

337. Uniform Trade Secrets Act § 1(2).
338. *Cuidado Casero Home Health of El Paso, Inc. v. Ayuda Home Health Care Servs., LLC*, 404 S.W.3d 737, 744 (Tex. App. 2013); *Bohnsack v. Varco, L.P.*, 668 F.3d 262, 279 (5th Cir. 2012).
339. *Astoria Indus. of Iowa, Inc. v. SNF, Inc.*, 223 S.W.3d 616, 634-35 (Tex. App. 2007); *Sands v. Estate of Buys*, 160 S.W.3d 684, 687-88 (Tex. App. 2005).
340. *Harrods Ltd. v. Sixty Internet Domain Names*, 110 F.Supp. 2d. 420 (E.D. Va. 2000).

domain name holder. This is especially useful against domain name owners who are difficult to find, or who reside outside of the U.S. Finally, the act allows trademark owners to elect to receive either actual damages or statutory damages of between USD 1,000 and 100,000 per domain name. These statutory damages can be obtained at any time, upon order of the court, before the termination of the suit. However, trademark owners cannot elect to receive statutory damages from "cybersquatters" who registered their domain names prior to the enactment of this new legislation.

§3. Dealer Termination

408. Unlike many foreign jurisdictions, U.S. law does not directly extend significant protection to dealers against termination. There is no general federal statute that grants certain rights to dealers in the event of a termination. In certain sectors of the economy, however, federal statutes extend some protection. There are federal statutes applicable to automobile dealers (15 U.S.C. sections 1221 et seq.), gasoline dealers (15 U.S.C. sections 2801 et seq.), agriculture (7 U.S.C. section 2303), soft drink bottlers (15 U.S.C. sections 135.01 et seq.). In addition, a number of states have enacted laws protecting dealers. For example, the Wisconsin Fair Dealership Law prohibits the termination of a dealership agreement without "good cause" (Wisconsin Statutes sections 135.01 et seq.).

409. The expansive scope of the federal and state franchise laws creates the possibility that a sales representative or a distributor be considered a "franchisee" under federal or state law. The legal implication of such a categorization is that the sales representative or dealer could be able to claim termination protection under the applicable franchisee statute even though the parties did not intend to establish a franchise relationship.

§4. Business Franchises

410. Franchises are regulated by both federal and state law. The FTC has adopted rules specifically applicable to "franchises." A franchise is defined as a continuing commercial relationship created by any arrangement whereby a person (i.e., the franchisee) is indirectly or directly required or advised to meet the quality standards prescribed by a franchisor, and the franchisee operates under a name using the trademark, service mark, trade name, advertising, or other commercial symbol designating the franchisor. In addition, the franchisor must exert or have the authority to exert a significant degree of control over the franchisee's method of operation such as the franchisee's business organization, promotional activities, management, marketing plan, or business affairs (16 C.F.R. Part 436.2). The term "franchise" does not include an agreement between a licensor and a single licensee to license a trademark, trade name, service mark, advertising, or other commercial symbol where such license is the only one of its general nature and type to be granted by the licensor with respect to that trademark, trade name, service mark, advertising, or other commercial symbols.

411. The franchise rules have taken greater importance due to the widespread use of the Internet. Franchises are frequently being offered over the Internet. Similarly, Internet businesses are being established as franchises.

412. The basic effect of the franchise rules is to require the franchisor or franchise broker to furnish the prospective franchisee with a significant amount of accurate information in a written document. The failure to provide this information is considered an unfair trade practice within the meaning of section 5 of the FTC Act (16 C.F.R. Part 436). The following is a list of some of the information that must be provided to the franchisee:

- The trademarks or other commercial symbols that identify the goods or services to be sold by the prospective franchisee.
- A factual description of the franchise offered to be sold by the franchisor.
- A statement of the total funds that must be paid by the franchisee to the franchisor in order to obtain or commence the franchise operation.
- A statement describing any recurring funds (e.g., royalties) required to be paid by the franchisee to the franchisor.
- A statement describing any real estate, services, supplies, products, inventories, signs, fixtures, or equipment relating to the establishment or the operation of the franchise business that the franchisee is directly or indirectly required by the franchisor to purchase, lease, or rent.
- A description of the basis for calculating, and, if such information is readily available, the actual amount of, any revenue or other consideration to be received by the franchisor from suppliers to the prospective franchisee in consideration for goods or services that the franchisor requires or advises the franchisee to obtain from such suppliers.

Chapter 4. State Regulation of the Conditions of Commercial Transactions

§1. Price and Supply Regulation

413. Although there are areas of the U.S. economy in which the prices that the market actors can charge for their products or services are regulated, there is no general price regulation that applies across all areas of the economy. However, one remnant of the common law that may be considered a regulation of prices is the concept of usury. This is generally defined as the charging of an excessive rate of interest for a loan or forbearance of money.[341] The purpose of the common law prohibition on usury is "to protect desperately poor people from the consequences of their own desperation."[342] Many states have enacted statutes prohibiting usury.[343] Although these laws vary slightly, the general elements are:

(1) the transaction must be a loan or a forbearance of money;
(2) the interest to be paid must exceed the maximum set by statute;
(3) the loan and interest must be absolutely payable, that is, not conditional;
(4) the lender must have a willful intent to enter into a usurious transaction.

§2. Consumer Law

I. Enforcement Agencies

414. Primary responsibility for the enforcement of consumer law in the U.S. lies with the FTC. The FTC Act gives the FTC broad enforcement authority over consumer protection issues. The FTC may prosecute any inquiry necessary to its duties in any part of the U.S. and may investigate the organization, business, conduct, practices, and management of any person, partnership, or corporation engaged in or whose business affects commerce, except banks, savings and loan institutions, federal credit unions and common carriers (15 U.S.C. sections 43, 46(a)).

II. Safety of Goods

415. The safety of goods is regulated in the U.S. through a combination of public and private enforcement. The Federal Food and Drug Administration is primarily responsible for the enforcement of the laws applicable to the safety of goods.

341. *Evans v. Harry Robinson Pontiac-Buick*, 983 S.W. 2d 946 (1999).
342. *Schneider v. Phelps*, 41 N.Y. 2d 238, 359 (1977).
343. Although there are some federal laws mandating maximum rates of interest regarding banks (*see*, e.g., the National Bank Act, 12 U.S.C. s. 12), usury law is mainly state law.

416. The U.S. legal system also relies on private litigants to ensure the safety of goods by the use of litigation against manufacturers and sellers of defective products. The general standard of product liability for manufacturers of defective products is "strict." In other words, if a defect exists the injured party does not have to prove that the manufacturer was negligent. The general rule is that a company that is in the business of selling or distributing products is subject to strict liability for harm to persons or property caused by a defective product that it sells.

417. There are three different types of defects according to the Restatement on Torts: A product is defective when, at the time of sale or distribution, it contains a manufacturing defect, a defect in design, or is defective because of inadequate instructions or warnings.[344] A manufacturing defect exists if the product departs from its intended design even though all possible care was exercised in the preparation and marketing of the product. In contrast, a product is defective in design if the foreseeable risks of harm posed by the product could have been reduced or avoided by the adoption of a reasonable alternative design by the seller or other distributors, and the omission of the alternative design renders the product not reasonably safe. Finally, a product is defective because of inadequate instructions or warnings when the foreseeable risks of harm posed by the product could have been reduced or avoided by the provision of reasonable instructions or warnings by the seller or other distributors, or a predecessor in the commercial chain of distribution, and the omission of the instructions or warnings renders the product not reasonably safe.[345]

418. The rule of strict product liability applies to the producer and the distributor of the products. Certain products, however, are comprised of various component parts that may or may not be produced by the same manufacturer and any of which may be defective. A company that produces or distributes a component is subject to liability for harm to persons or property caused by a product into which the component is integrated if the component is defective in itself and the defect causes the harm.[346] In addition, the component producer or distributor may be liable under a products liability theory if: (1) it substantially participates in the integration of the component into the design of the product; (2) the integration of the component causes the product to be defective; and (3) the defect in the product causes the harm.

419. Another issue that commonly arises concerns the liability of a business that acquires the business that produced or distributed the defective product or component. In this case, the liability of the successor business depends on the nature of the acquisition. Liability will generally result if one of four conditions are met:[347]

344. Restatement Torts: Products Liability (Third) s. 2.
345. *Id.*
346. Restatement Torts: Products Liability (Third) s. 5.
347. *Id.*, s. 12.

(1) the parties agree that the successor will assume such liability;
(2) the acquisition results from a fraudulent conveyance to escape liability for the debts or liabilities of the predecessor;
(3) the acquisition constitutes a consolidation or merger with the predecessor; or
(4) the acquisition results in the successor becoming a continuation of the predecessor.

420. In many instances, the conduct of the injured party may have contributed to the injury. In such cases, the recovery of damages may be reduced if the conduct of the injured party combined with the product defect to cause the harm and the injured party's conduct fails to conform to generally applicable rules establishing appropriate standards of care.[348] The manner and extent of the reduction will depend on the particular state law and case law applicable to the case.

421. Product liability cases generally revolve around the issue of causation. The courts have developed certain inferences to prove causation. It may be inferred that the harm was caused by a product defect existing at the time of sale or distribution, without proof of a specific defect, under two conditions:[349]

(1) the incident that harmed the plaintiff was of a kind that ordinarily occurs as a result of product defect; and
(2) the incident that harmed the plaintiff was not, in the particular case, solely the result of causes other than product defect existing at the time of sale or distribution.

III. Sales Promotion and Commercial Practices

422. The FTC has primary responsibility for policing sales promotion and advertising practices. The FTC has the general authority to prohibit "unfair or deceptive acts or practices" (15 U.S.C. section 45). It also has the specific authority to prohibit misleading claims relating to foods, drugs, medical devices, services, and cosmetics (15 U.S.C. sections 52 et seq.).[350]

423. The concepts of deception and unfairness are two separate but related concepts. According to the FTC, a sales promotion is deceptive if: (1) it contains a misrepresentation or omission; (2) that is likely to mislead consumers acting reasonably under the circumstances; and (3) to their detriment.[351]

---

348. *Id.*, s. 17.
349. *Id.*, s. 3.
350. The Federal Drug Administration (FDA) is responsible for food labeling. Working Agreement between the FTC and FDA, 3 Trade Reg. Rep. (CCH) 9851 (1971).
351. Deception Policy Statement, 103 F.T.C. 174 (1984).

424. A sales promotion is unfair if it: (1) causes or is likely to cause substantial consumer injury; (2) which is not reasonably avoidable by consumers themselves; and (3) is not outweighed by countervailing benefits to consumers or competition.[352]

425. Under section 18 of the FTC Act (15 U.S.C. section 57a) the Commission is authorized to prescribe "rules which define with specificity acts or practices which are unfair or deceptive acts or practices in or affecting commerce within the meaning of section 5(a)(1) of the Act." The FTC has issued rules and guides that provide guidance as to the application of the rules to particular industries by identifying specific acts or practices that the FTC considers to be unfair or deceptive:

- Guides for the Nursery Industry (16 C.F.R. Part 18).
- Guides for the Rebuilt, Reconditioned and Other Used Automobile Parts Industry (16 C.F.R. Part 20).
- Guides for the Jewelry, Precious Metals, and Pewter Industries (16 C.F.R. Part 23).
- Guides for Select Leather and Imitation Leather Products (16 C.F.R. Part 24).
- Tire Advertising and Labeling Guides (16 C.F.R. Part 228).
- Guides Against Deceptive Pricing (16 C.F.R. Part 233).
- Guides Against Bait Advertising (16 C.F.R. Part 238).
- Guides for the Advertising of Warranties and Guarantees (16 C.F.R. Part 239).
- Guides for the Household Furniture Industry (16 C.F.R. Part 250).
- Guide Concerning Use of the Word "Free" and Similar Representations (16 C.F.R. Part 251).
- Guides for Private Vocational and Distance Education Schools (16 C.F.R. Part 254).
- Guides Concerning Use of Endorsements and Testimonials in Advertising (16 C.F.R. Part 255).
- Guides Concerning Fuel Economy Advertising for New Automobiles (16 C.F.R. Part 259).
- Guides for the Use of Environmental Marketing Claims (16 C.F.R. Part 260).
- Rules and Regulations Under the Wool Products Labeling Act of 1939 (16 C.F.R. Part 300).
- Rules and Regulations Under Fur Products Labeling Act (16 C.F.R. Part 301).
- Rules and Regulations Under the Textile Fiber Products Identification Act (16 C.F.R. Part 303).
- Rule Concerning Disclosures Regarding Energy Consumption and Water Use of Certain Home Appliances and Other Products Required Under the Energy Policy and Conservation Act (16 C.F.R. Part 305).
- Rule Concerning Automotive Fuel Ratings, Certification and Posting (16 C.F.R. Part 306).
- Labeling Requirements for Alternative Fuels and Alternative Fueled Vehicles (16 C.F.R. Part 309).
- Telemarketing Sales Rule (16 C.F.R. Part 310).

352. Unfairness Policy Statement, 104 F.T.C. 1070 (1984).

- Deceptive Advertising as to Sizes of Viewable Pictures Shown by Television Receiving Sets (16 C.F.R. Part 410).
- Retail Food Store Advertising and Marketing Practices (16 C.F.R. Part 424).
- Use of Prenotification Negative Option Plans (16 C.F.R. Part 425).
- Power Output Claims for Amplifiers Utilized in Home Entertainment Products (16 C.F.R. Part 432).
- Preservation of Consumers' Claims and Defenses (16 C.F.R. Part 433).
- Mail or Telephone Order Merchandise Rule (16 C.F.R. Part 435).
- Credit Practices Rule (16 C.F.R. Part 444).
- Used Motor Vehicle Trade Regulation Rule (16 C.F.R. Part 455).
- Labeling and Advertising of Home Insulation (16 C.F.R. Part 460).
- Interpretations of Magnuson-Moss Warranty Act (16 C.F.R. Part 700).
- Disclosure of Written Consumer Product Warranty Terms and Conditions (16 C.F.R. Part 701).
- Pre-Sale Availability of Written Warranty Terms (16 C.F.R. Part 702).
- Informal Dispute Settlement Procedures (16 C.F.R. Part 703).

426. To remedy a deceptive or unfair practice, the FTC has several remedies at its disposal. It has the authority to issue a cease-and-desist order to end the deceptive or unfair practice. In the alternative or in addition, the FTC has the authority to compel corrective advertising to dispel the misconceptions created by the misleading advertising. The jurisdiction of the FTC extends extraterritorially to practices that harm U.S. consumers.[353]

427. The general policy of the FTC is that an advertiser must have a reasonable basis for making claims before those claims are disseminated.[354] For claims related to health or safety, the FTC applies heightened scrutiny. In such cases, the FTC requires competent and reliable scientific evidence. Liability for unsubstantiated claims is strict. In other words, the FTC does not have to prove the intent to deceive or mislead.

428. Sales promotion efforts via the Internet are being treated in much the same way as traditional means of sales promotion. In fact, the increasing reliance on the Internet and the relatively low costs of advertising on the Internet has compelled the FTC to increase its enforcement efforts in this sector.

The practice of unsolicited e-mail marketing (commonly referred to as spam) has not been regulated at the federal level yet. There are several bills pending before Congress that have a strong likelihood of being adopted. Over half of the states have adopted some form of legislation directed at unsolicited commercial e-mail.[355] These laws have a broad jurisdictional scope as they typically apply if the recipient

353. *FTC v. Skybiz.com*, 57 Fed. Appx. 374 (10 Cir. 2003); *FTC v. Magui Publishers*, 1993 WL 430102 (9th Cir. 1993).
354. *Thompson Medical Co.*, 104 F.T.C. 839 (1984); *Pfizer, Inc.*, 81 F.T.C. 23 (1972).
355. *See*, e.g., s. 815 Ill. Comp. Stat. 511/1 to 511/10 (2002).

of the unsolicited communication is a resident of that state regardless of the location of the sender.[356] Certain narrow exceptions are common such as the existence of a prior business relationship, the request or consent of the recipient and e-mail to some free accounts.

429. In addition to federal law on unfair trade practices, all of the individual states have their own legislation. All but two of these states (Iowa and North Dakota) offer a private right of action for violations of their laws.

IV. Consumer Warranties

430. The Magnuson-Moss Warranty Act requires any warrantor warranting a consumer product to a consumer by means of a written warranty to fully and conspicuously disclose in simple language the terms and conditions of such warranty (15 U.S.C. section 2302(a)). The act applies to "consumer products," that is, "any tangible personal property which is normally used for personal, family or household purposes" (15 U.S.C. section 5614(1)). For example, fire sprinklers purchased for installation in a commercial building are not consumer products even though the same types of sprinklers may be used in residential buildings.[357] The term "warrantor" means any supplier or other persons who gives or offers to give a written warranty or who is or may be obligated under an implied warranty. The term "consumer" means a buyer (other than for purposes of resale) of any consumer products, any person to whom such product is transferred during the term of an implied or written warranty applicable to the product, and any other person who is entitled by the terms of such warranty or under applicable state law to enforce against the warrantor the obligations of the warranty (15 U.S.C. section 2301). This federal law only applies to warranties for consumer products costing the consumer more than USD 5.

431. The Magnuson-Moss Warranty Act does not require the seller of a product to provide a written warranty. Instead, it requires the warranty on consumer goods to include the following items:

- the clear identification of the names and addresses of the warrantors;
- the identity of the party or parties to whom the warranty is extended;
- the products or parts covered;
- a statement of what the warrantor will do in the event of a defect, malfunction, or failure to conform with such written warranty;
- a statement of what the consumer must do and expenses he must bear to benefit from the warranty;
- exceptions and exclusions from the terms of the warranty.

---

356. *See*, e.g., Del. Code. tit. 11. ss. 937(4), 938(b).
357. *State of Illinois v. Central Sprinkles Corp.*, 2001–2 CCH Trade Cases 73,514 (C.D. Ill. 2001).

432. The Act requires that warranties must be labeled as either "full" or "limited." A "full" warranty is one which: (1) provides a remedy within a reasonable time without charge; (2) imposes no limits on implied warranties; (3) makes a conspicuous disclosure of any limitations on damages; (4) provides a refund or replacement if warrantor is unable to repair after a reasonable attempt; and (5) requires only notification in order to obtain a remedy (15 U.S.C. section 2301(1)). All other warranties are considered "limited" and must be labeled as such. However, a limited warranty may not restrict implied warranties such implied warranty of merchantability to terms less than a written limited warranty (15 U.S.C. section 2302(8)(b)).

433. In order for a warrantor of a consumer product by means of a written warranty to meet the federal minimum standards for warranty, the warrantor must remedy the defect or malfunction within a reasonable time (15 U.S.C. section 2304). If the product (or a component part thereof) contains a defect or malfunction after a reasonable number of attempts by the warrantor to remedy defects or malfunctions in such product, such warrantor must permit the consumer to elect either a refund for or replacement without charge of such products or part (as the case may be). It is possible for the warrantor to preclude liability for consequential damages if the limiting language is "conspicuous" on the face of the warranty.[358]

V. Duty of Good Faith

434. Every contract imposes upon each party a duty of good faith and fair dealing in its performance and its enforcement.[359] Defining this duty can be a difficult task. For merchants, this duty means "honesty in fact and the observance of reasonable commercial standards of fair dealing in the trade" (UCC section 2-103(1)(b)).

VI. Standardized Terms and Adhesion Contracts

435. Unlike many civil law countries, the U.S. does not have a consumer protection law specifically applicable to standardized contracts.[360] The general rule is that a party that signs a standardized contract is bound to the terms of that agreement.[361] However, if one party has reason to believe that the other party is unaware of a particular term in the standardized contract and, had he or she known, he or she would not have signed the contract, then that particular term is not part of the agreement.[362]

358. *Najran v. Fleetwood Enterprises, Inc.*, 659 F.Supp. 1031 (1986).
359. Restatement Contracts (Second) s. 205; *Sterling Nat. Mortgage Co. v. Mortgage Corner*, 97 F.3d 39 (1996).
360. Dugan, *Standardized Form Contracts*, 24 *Wayne L. Rev.* 1307 (1978):.
361. Restatement Contracts (Second) s. 211(a).
362. *Id.*, s. 211(c).

VII. Unconscionability

436. Another common law doctrine that operates to protect consumers is the rule of unconscionability. According to the Supreme Court, a contract or a term of a contract is unconscionable if "no man in his senses and not under delusion would make on the one hand, and as no honest and fair man would accept on the other."[363] If a contract or term of a contract is considered unconscionable, the court may refuse to enforce the contract or the particular term. However, the unconscionability doctrine, which is used as a defense, is rarely successful.

VIII. Sales Below-Cost

437. Selling at below-cost prices is not in itself illegal. This practice may, however, be deemed illegal if combined with unlawful intent. For example, sales at below-cost-prices are illegal if used as an instrument to destroy a competitor. A flat prohibition on sales below-cost regardless of the purpose or intent of the practice may be unconstitutional.[364]

438. A number of states have enacted laws prohibiting sales below-cost when combined with an anticompetitive intent. The basic purpose of such laws is to protect small competitors who are not able to compete with such practices because of their inability to subsidize the loss-making operations with a profit-making operation.[365] For the very same reason, some state statutes prohibit the practice of giving products away without cost. A number of states also have laws prohibiting sales at below-cost prices in specific industries, for example, liquor, dairy products, and cigarettes.

439. Perhaps the most important, but yet most difficult aspect of this offense is determining the cost of acquiring or making a product or service. In general, the calculation of cost is determined by the particular statute. These laws identify the particular costs that may be factored into the analysis.

IX. Packaging and Labeling

440. The federal government and the states have enacted legislation dealing with the labeling of products, including, for example, food products, automobiles, agricultural commodities, drugs and poisons, fabrics, hazardous substances, imported goods, insecticides, and liquor.[366] In enacting the Fair Packaging and Labeling Act (15 U.S.C sections 1451–1461), Congress declared that informed consumers are essential to the fair and efficient functioning of a free market economy and that

363. *Hume v. United States*, 132 U.S. 406 (1889).
364. *State ex rel. Anderson v. Fleming Co.*, 339 P. 2d 12 (1959).
365. *Baseline Liquors v. Cicle K Corp.*, 630 P. 2d 38 (1981).
366. *State v. W.S. Buck Mercantile Co.*, 264 P. 1023 (1928).

packages and their labels should enable consumers to obtain accurate information as to the quantity of the contents and should facilitate value comparisons (15 U.S.C section 1451).

441. Packaged consumer commodities distributed in commerce must meet regulations established by the federal Department of Health and Human Services if the consumer commodity is food, drug, device, or cosmetic. Other products fall under the jurisdiction of the FTC (15 U.S.C section 1454).

442. In general, the label must identify the commodity and the name and place of business of the manufacturer, packer, or distributor. The net quantity of contents (in terms of weight, measure, or numerical count) must be separately and accurately stated in a uniform location upon the principal display panel of the label. If there is a separate label statement of net quantity of contents on or affixed to the package, it must appear in conspicuous and easily legible type in distinct contrast with other matter on the package. If there is a representation as to the number of servings, the label must contain a statement of the net quantity (in terms of weight, measure, or numerical count) of each serving.

443. The statute defines the Department of Health and Human Services and the FTC rule-making authority (15 U.S.C section 1454) and rule-making procedure (15 U.S.C section 1455). Any consumer commodity that is a food, drug, device, or cosmetic and that is introduced or delivered for introduction into commerce in violation of the statute or regulations thereunder is misbranded within the meaning of the Food, Drug, and Cosmetic Act. Any violation of the statute or regulations with respect to other consumer commodities is an unfair or deceptive trade practice in violation of the FTC Act (15 U.S.C section 1456(b)). In the case of imported consumer commodities, the statute is enforced by the Secretary of the Treasury (15 U.S.C section 1456(c)).

444. There are a number of federal laws that are applicable to specific industries. For example, there is the Textile Fiber Products Identification Act, (15 U.S.C sections 70–70k), Wool Products Labeling Act (15 U.S.C sections 68–68j) and the Fur Products Labeling Act (15 U.S.C sections 69–69j). With certain exceptions, the Cigarette Labeling and Advertising Act (15 U.S.C. sections 1331–1339) makes it unlawful to manufacture, import, or package for sale or distribution within the U.S. any cigarettes the package of which fails to bear one of the labels required by statute, located in a conspicuous place on every cigarette package and appearing in conspicuous and legible type in contrast by typography, layout, or color with other printed matter on the package (15 U.S.C. section 1333). No other statement relating to smoking and health may be required on any cigarette package, (15 U.S.C. section 1334(a)) nor may any requirement or prohibition based on smoking and health be imposed under state law with respect to the advertising or promotion of any cigarettes, the packages of which are labeled in conformity with the act (15 U.S.C. section 1334(b)).

X. Privacy Laws

445. The privacy rights of individuals and businesses are regulated by a pot-pourri of federal and state laws that fall into two general categories.[367] The first group of laws has as their specific purpose the protection of privacy. Examples of this type of law would be: Children's Online Privacy Protection Act[368] Family Education Rights and Privacy Act,[369] Gramm-Leach-Bliley Financial Services Act,[370] and California Consumer Privacy Act.[371] The second group of laws are not specifically directed at the protection of privacy but have been extended by statutory amendment or interpretation to protect privacy rights. Examples of this latter set of laws would be Cable Communications Policy Act,[372] Fair Credit Reporting Act,[373] and the FTC Act.[374]

446. Supplementing the federal statutes are rules promulgated by the FTC such as the Red Flags Rule requiring financial institutions to have identity theft prevention programs, the COPPA Rule requiring websites and apps to get parental consent before collecting personal information from children, the Telemarking Sales Rule limiting the hours that telemarketers may call consumers, and the Disposal Rule requiring companies to properly dispose of credit reports and information derived from them.

447. In addition to the federal laws directly and indirectly regulating privacy, there are many state privacy and data security laws governing the collection, use, protection, and disclosure of personal information. Many states have adopted "baby FTC Acts" resembling the federal FTC Act containing broad consumer protections and prohibitions on unfair or deceptive business practices, data breach and security laws, credit card transaction laws, records disposal laws, and medical information laws.

A. *Personal Health Information*

448. Although the U.S. has not had a unified approach to privacy, it has for over two decades given particular emphasis to protecting personal health information. The Health Insurance Portability and Accountability Act of 1996 (HIPAA) regulates what health care providers and health plans do with personally identifiable

367. The Constitution recognizes a general privacy right to personal information. *NASA v. Nelson*, 131 S.Ct. 746 (2011).
368. 15 U.S.C. ss. 6501–06.
369. 20 U.S.C. s. 1232g.
370. 15 U.S.C. ss. 6801 et seq.
371. Available at https://leginfo.legislature.ca.gov/faces/billTextClient.xhtml?bill_id=201720180AB375.
372. 47 U.S.C. s. 551.
373. 15 U.S.C. ss. 1681–1681u.
374. 15 U.S.C. s. 45.

information. HIPAA also extends to the "business associates" of these covered entities. The term "business associate" refers to a person or entity that performs certain services, functions, or activities for or on behalf of a covered entity that involve the use or disclosure of personal health information. For example, a business associate would include the following services performed for a covered entity:

- Health insurance claims processing and administration.
- Data analysis and processing.
- Quality assurance.
- Health benefits management.

449. HIPAA and the rules promulgated under the federal statute require imposing limits on what the covered entities and the business associates can do with the personal health information. Covered entities and their business associates must only use the minimum amount of personal health information necessary to complete a transaction. They are also required to adopt and maintain data security procedures, protocols, and policies to protect the personal health information which they collect. In there is a security breach, HIPAA requires the covered entities and their business associates to notify the affected individuals.

B. Gramm-Leach-Bliley Financial Services Act

450. The Gramm-Leach-Bliley Financial Services Act prevents financial institutions from disclosing to a nonaffiliated third party any "nonpublic personal information,"[375] unless such financial institution provides or has provided to the consumer an adequate notice. The term "financial institution" includes credit reporting agencies.[376] The term "nonaffiliated third party" means any entity that is not an affiliate of, or related by common ownership or affiliated by corporate control with, the particular financial institution. Before any disclosure to a nonaffiliated third party occurs, the financial institution must clearly and conspicuously provide notice to the consumer that such information may be disclosed to such third party. In addition, the consumer must be given the opportunity to direct that such information not be disclosed to such third party and an explanation of how the consumer can exercise that nondisclosure option.

451. The Gramm-Leach-Bliley Financial Services Act does not prohibit the disclosure of nonpublic personal information with the consent of the consumer or as necessary to effect, administer, or enforce a transaction requested or authorized by the consumer, or in connection with servicing or processing a financial product or service requested or authorized by the consumer. Moreover, financial institutions are

375. The term "nonpublic personal information" means personally identifiable financial information: (i) provided by a consumer to a financial institution; (ii) resulting from any transaction with the consumer or any service performed for the consumer; or (iii) otherwise obtained by the financial institution.

376. *Trans Union LLC v. FTC*, 295 F.3d 42 (D.C. Cir. 2002).

permitted to disclose personal information to comply with federal, state, or local laws, rules, or to comply with a civil, criminal, or regulatory investigation.

452. The Gramm-Leach-Bliley Financial Services Act also imposes an ongoing notice obligation on the financial institutions. At the time of establishing a customer relationship with a consumer, and not less than annually during the continuation of such relationship, financial institutions are required to provide clear and conspicuous disclosure to such consumers of such a financial institution's privacy policies and practices.

C. Federal Trade Commission Act

453. The FTC Act does not explicitly protect privacy. Instead, the FTC Act[377] contains a general clause that simply prohibits "unfair methods of competition in or affecting commerce, and unfair or deceptive acts or practices in or affecting commerce."[378] The FTC has used this general prohibition on unfair commercial practices to protect the privacy rights of consumers. For example, even though the FTC Act does not affirmatively require companies to have a privacy policy, the FTC has taken the position if a company discloses a privacy policy, the failure to comply with it constitutes a violation of the FTC Act.[379]

454. The FTC has used the broad language of the FTC Act against companies and individuals who have made misleading public statements regarding their privacy policies. For example, the FTC investigated and settled a case against the online advertising company, Turn, Inc., used consumer information even after the customers opted out of allowing Turn, Inc. to use their data.

455. The FTC Act provides monetary penalties of up to USD 41,484 per offense and criminal sanctions of imprisonment for up to ten years.

456. The FTC Act also plays an important role in international data protection and privacy efforts. The European Data Privacy Regulation prohibits the transfer of personal data from the EU non-EU Member States that do not offer an adequate

377. 15 U.S.C. s. 45.
378. The law does not apply to unfair methods of competition involving commerce with foreign nations (other than import commerce) unless such methods of competition have a direct, substantial, and reasonably foreseeable effect on commerce which is not commerce with foreign nations, or on import commerce with foreign nations; or on export commerce with foreign nations, of a person engaged in such commerce in the U.S.; and such effect gives rise to a claim under s. 5 of the FTC Act.
379. *See Federal Trade Commission v. Wyndham Worldwide Corp.*, 10 F.Supp. 3d 602 (D.N.J. 2014), *aff'd*, 799 F.3d 236 (3rd Cir. 2015).

level of protection.[380] The U.S.–EU Privacy Shield is considered by the Commission to offer an adequate level of protection.[381] Compliance with the Privacy Shield requires companies to submit a statement to the U.S. Department of Commerce that they comply with the Privacy Shield principles. The U.S. FTC has the authority under the FTC Act to prosecute companies who fail to comply with the declaration. For example, the FTC pursued claims against Google after Google launched its social network "Google Buzz," declared compliance with the safe harbor principles but failed to observe them.[382]

D. Data Security

457. Similar to data privacy, the FTC Act does not specifically address data security. The FTC is forced to protect consumers against data theft by applying the general prohibition on unfair commercial practices. Some examples of enforcement actions brought by the FTC alleging that the failure to take reasonable and appropriate steps to protect personal information is an unfair act or practice are as follows:

- Where the company failed to use readily accessible security measures to limit access to customer data.
- Where the company failed to maintain sufficient measures to detect unauthorized access or conduct security investigations.
- Where the company failed to encrypt information while it was in transit or stored on in-store networks.
- Where the company stored personally identifiable information in a file format that permitted anonymous access.
- Where the company stored information longer than necessary and thereby increasing the risk of theft.

E. Cable Communications Policy Act

458. The Cable Communications Policy Act[383] prohibits a cable operator from disclosing personally identifiable information[384] concerning any subscriber without the prior consent of that subscriber. It also requires cable operators to take such

380. Regulation (EU) 2016/679 of the European Parliament and of the Council of 27 April 2016 on the protection of natural persons with regard to the processing of personal data and on the free movement of such data, and repealing Directive 95/46/EC (General Data Protection Regulation) (Text with EEA relevance) O.J. 2016 (L 119) 1.
381. Commission Implementing Decision (EU) 2016/1250 of 12 July 2016 pursuant to Directive 95/46/EC of the European Parliament and of the Council on the adequacy of the protection provided by the EU-U.S. Privacy Shield, O.J. 2016 (L 207) 1.
382. *In re Google, Inc.*, FTC File No. 102 3136 (Mar. 30, 2011).
383. 47 U.S.C. s. 551.
384. The term "personally identifiable information" does not include any record of aggregate data which does not identify particular persons.

actions as are necessary to prevent unauthorized access to such information by a person other than the subscriber or cable operator. However, a cable operator is allowed to disclose such information if the disclosure is necessary to provide a cable service or made pursuant to a court order authorizing such disclosure.

459. Moreover, the cable operator must grant cable subscriber access to all personally identifiable information regarding that subscriber, which is collected and maintained by a cable operator. Such information must be made available to the subscriber at reasonable times and at a convenient place designated by such cable operator. A cable subscriber shall be provided reasonable opportunity to correct any error in such information.

F. Children's Online Privacy Protection Act (COPPA)

460. The Children's Online Privacy Protection Act[385] makes it unlawful for an operator of a website or online service directed to children,[386] or any operator that has actual knowledge that it is collecting personal information from a child (i.e., an individual under the age of 13) to provide notice on the website of what information is collected from children by the operator, how the operator uses such information, and the operator's disclosure practices for such information and to obtain verifiable parental consent for the collection, use, or disclosure of personal information from children.[387] The term "operator" means any person who operates a website located on the Internet or an online service and who collects or maintains personal information from or about the users of or visitors to such website or online service, or on whose behalf such information is collected or maintained, where such website or online service is operated for commercial purposes. The term "personal information" encompasses the first and last name of the person, a home or other physical address, an e-mail address, a telephone number or a Social Security number. Consent is not required in the case of online contact information collected from a child that is used only to respond directly on a one-time basis to a specific request from the child and is not used to recontact the child and is not maintained in retrievable form by the operator.

385. 15 U.S.C. ss. 6501–06.
386. A website is directed to children if it is a commercial website or online service that is targeted to children.
387. The term "disclosure" means, with respect to personal information the release of personal information collected from a child in identifiable form by an operator for any purpose, except where such information is provided to a person other than the operator who provides support for the internal operations of the website and does not disclose or use that information for any other purpose and making personal information collected from a child by a website or online service directed to children, publicly available in identifiable form, by any means including by a public posting, through the Internet.

Selected Bibliography

American Bar Association. *Guide to Credit and Bankruptcy*. Chicago: American Bar Association, 2009.

Anderman, Steven D. *Interface Between Intellectual Property Rights and Competition Policy*. Cambridge: Cambridge University Press, 2007.

Andersen, William R. *Antitrust Law: Policy and Practice*. 3rd ed. New York: C Paul Rogers Publisher, 1999.

Areeda, Phillip. *Antitrust Law: An Analysis of Antitrust Principles and Their Application*. 2nd ed. Boston: Little, Brown, 2000.

Bebchuk, Lucian A. *Freedom of Contract and the Corporation: An Essay On the Mandatory Role of Corporate Law*. Cambridge: Cambridge University Press, 1988.

Broder, Douglas. *U.S. Antitrust Law and Enforcement*. Oxford: Oxford University Press, 2010.

Calabresi, Guido. *A Common Law for the Age of Statutes*. Cambridge: Harvard University Press, 1982.

Cary, William Lucius. *Cases and Materials On Corporations*. 7th ed. Mineola: West Publishing, 1995.

Cox, James D. *Corporations*. New York: Aspen Law & Business, 1997.

Currie, David. "The Constitution and the Supreme Court: The Protection of Economic Interests", *The University of Chicago Law Review* 52 (1985): 324.

Domowitz, Ian. *Two Hundred Years of Bankruptcy: A Tale of Legislation and Economic Fluctuations*. Evanston: Northwestern Press, 1997.

Friedland, Jerold. *Understanding International Business and Financial Transactions*. 2nd ed., 2005.

Halpern, Sheldon W. *Fundamentals of United States Intellectual Property Law: Copyright, Patent, and Trademark*. Boston: Northeastern Press, 1999.

Hart, Frederick M. *Negotiable Instruments Under the Uniform Commercial Code*. New York: J. Wiley & Sons, 1997.

Hawkland, William D. *Problems and Materials on Commercial Paper and Banking*. Westbury: The Foundation Press, 1995.

Hillman, Robert A. *Common Law and Equity under the Uniform Commercial Code*. Boston: Warren, Gorham & Lamont, 1985.

Holmes, Oliver Wendell. *The Common Law*. Boston: Little Brown, 1923.

Hüpkes, Eva H. G. *The Legal Aspects of Bank Insolvency: A Comparative Analysis of Western Europe, the United States and Canada*. New York: Palgrave Macmillan, 2000.

Selected Bibliography

Jordan, Robert L. *Commercial Paper.* 2nd ed. Mineola: Foundation Press, 1987.

Lawrence, William. *Understanding Negotiable Instruments and Payment Systems.* New York: Matthew Bender, 2002.

Lawrence, William. *Understanding Secured Transactions.* 4th ed. New York: Matthew Bender, 2007.

Leaffer, Marshall. *Understanding Copyright Law.* 4th ed. New York: Matthew Bender, 2005.

Maggs, Peter B. *Internet and Computer Law: Cases, Comments, Questions.* St. Paul: West Group, 2001.

McCaffrey, Stephen. *Understanding International Law.* New York: Matthew Bender, 2006.

McDowell, Gary L. *Language of Law and the Foundations of American Constitutionalism.* Cambridge: Cambridge University Press, 2010.

O'Kelley, Charles R. *Corporations and Other Business Associations: Cases and Materials.* 2nd ed. Boston: Little, Brown, 1996.

Oakley, John & Vikram Amar. *American Civil Procedure.* New York: N & L Publishers, 2009.

Paust, Jordan J. *International Law as Law of the United States.* Durham: Carolina Academic Press, 1996.

Posner, Richard A. *Antitrust Law: An Economic Perspective.* Chicago: University Of Chicago Press, 1976.

Redlich, Norman, John Attanasio & Joel Goldstein. *Understanding Constitutional Law.* 3rd ed., 2005.

Roebuck, Derek. *The Background of the Common Law.* 2nd ed. New York: Oxford University Press, 1990.

Siegen, Bernard H. *Economic Liberties and the Constitution.* Chicago: University of Chicago Press, 1980.

Index

The numbers here refer to paragraph numbers.

Index

Index